MW00961048

DAVID S.
AND
CATHERINE T.
MAYNARD

SEATTLE PIONEERS

TWO OF THE OREGON *IMMIGRANTS* of 1850

By THOMAS W. PROSCH,

SEATTLE, 1906.

COPYRIGHT 2014 BIG BYTE BOOKS

Get more great reading from BIG BYTE BOOKS

Contents

DAVID SWINSON "DOC" MAYNARD

His Birth, Ancestry, Education.

MARCH 22d, 1808, a child was born at or near the town of Castleton, Rutland County, in the State of Vermont, to whom was given the name David Swinson Maynard, the middle name being the family name on the side of his mother. The Maynards and the Swinsons were of strong American stock. The two families had long been acquainted, having lived in the same neighborhood, fought in the same wars, educated and reared their children together, intermarried, and otherwise associated in the many ways incident to the life and times of the eighteenth century, first in the British Province and later in the young American possession and State in which their lots had been cast. It is related that one of the young Maynards and one of the young Swinsons, both of whom became progenitors of the boy referred to in the opening sentence, were impressed on a British ship, commanded by Capt. Burgoyne, at the outbreak of the Revolutionary war. When they signified their desire to go on shore they were forcibly detained, and were told that King George needed their services, and intended to have them, in putting down the rebellion recently inaugurated by their countrymen in Massachusetts and other Colonies. Swinson and Maynard counselled together, and at length succeeded in leaving the ship in the darkness, with nothing but their underclothing,

1

barefooted, getting on land wet, cold and all but exhausted. A Scotch woman, who could talk Gaelic only, befriended them, and with her help they were enabled to reach the camp of General Washington, where both enlisted in the Continental army, in which they remained to the end of the long struggle then in the days of its beginning.

David S. Maynard had three sisters. All were educated as well as the schools of the day permitted. With the sisters, however, this memoir has no more to do. When his course in the schools had been completed, young Maynard began the study of medicine. Dr. Woodward was his instructor, the boy serving in the doctor's office and giving general help while acquiring the information needed for the practise of his chosen profession. Upon completing his time and course the young physician was given a diploma, and for forty-four years following was in more or less active practice. Presumably his services were not much sought or richly compensated in the community where he had been reared, for he soon after moved west, settling in Lorain County, Ohio, and doing business in and near Cleveland, then a place of four or five thousand inhabitants, now a city with one hundred times as many.

BEFORE going to Ohio, though, the student and doctor had adventures and troubles such as usually fall to the lot of active, promising young men. In his first love affair there was a misunderstanding and a failure. The young lady is said to have been most winning and lovable. In nowise

2

discouraged, Maynard promptly paid court to another girl, and in 1828, on the 28th of August, at twenty years of age, he and Lydia A. Rickey were married. Shortly afterwards they left Vermont for the place on Lake Erie that has since become the seventh city in population in the United States. At the new home, a few miles west of Cleveland, two children were born to them—a son, Henry C., and a daughter, Frances J., who subsequently became Mrs. Patterson, and is still living.

There the couple dwelt more than a score of years. He was energetic, and he made efforts and investments in various directions. Of these the most notable was the establishment of a medical school, in which at one time were one hundred and fifty students. With him in this enterprise were Doctors Mauzey and Ackley. Beginning about that time and extending up to the period of civil war, there was much trouble with the currency, and in 1837 occurred a great financial crash and crisis, in which the business of the nation was rent and broken as never before, the effects upon the people being direful indeed. The banks were nearly all closed, few ever again being reopened, and the banks that succeeded them for twenty years had smaller deposits than had the banks that had failed in 1837. And this while Ohio was rapidly increasing in population. The resultant loss of confidence, the lack of money and the bad trade conditions generally prevalent made it exceedingly difficult for men to carry on their commercial undertakings. Especially was this true of men like Maynard, who were free and open-handed, helpful of others, careless of the morrow, and who were heavily leaned upon by acquaintances in the support of their schemes. Maynard became responsible for another man to the extent of $30,000. The business failed, and in the wreck Maynard was financially ruined. It was impossible for him there to recover, and he began to look longingly towards California as the region of future hope and wealth. In 1849 there had been a great rush of men by water and land to the new region of gold. In this he had been unable to join, but he now resolved to be among those who would go the following year. In coming to this determination he was moved also by the disaffection of his wife, whose nagging and faultfinding had become well-nigh unendurable. He collected such moneys as he could, simplified his affairs, and fixed his wife and two now grown children as comfortably as possible, leaving everything to them but the merest pittance. He might have gone to California more easily and quickly by steamer, but it would have cost him about five hundred dollars, and he felt that he could not afford it either on his own account or that of his family. He believed that he could work his way across the continent without money, by making himself useful to other immigrants, and that, under the circumstances, it was his duty to do this way if he went.

A LONG AND PERILOUS JOURNEY

OF the five months' journey to the Pacific the Doctor left account in his diary, which is used in the pages following. It was evidently inconvenient to him to write, as the daily spaces were small, three to the page, and there was much to do on the way, but between the lines and the times much can now be seen and read that does not appear in letters and words upon the paper. The first entry is that of Tuesday, April 9, 1850, here given:

Left home for California. Passed through Norwalk to Monroeville. Took the cars to Sandusky. Saw a large eagle on the prairie. Passage, 75 cents. Paid to Drakeley, $4. Dinner and horsefeed, 75 cents. Total, $5.50.

There are no more entries until April 20th, at Cincinnati, from which it may be inferred that the traveler was about eleven days in making the trip across the State from north to south, probably on his horse, which he also probably sold at Cincinnati. The second and third diary notes are these:

April 20th.—Left Cincinnati at 4 o'clock on board the Natchez.

April 21st.—Arrived at Louisville at 10. Walked to New Albany, in Indiana, a place of about 7,000 inhabitants— Lockville. Saw James Porter, the Kentucky giant, 7 2-3 feet.

The Doctor journeyed on without making notes until the middle of May, by which time he had arranged fully for the long remainder of the trip. He had a mule, a buffalo robe, a gun, a few medicines, his surgical instruments and several books. He connected himself with a party, depending upon his wits, his professional skill, his talent for doing things, his good humor and his general usefulness wherever placed, to carry him through to the other shore in safety and reasonable comfort. That his ideas were correctly based is well known, and to a certain extent are portrayed in the narrative following from his own pencil:

Thursday, May 16.—Crossed the Missouri river at Saint Joseph, and encamped.

May 17.—Left camp about 11 o'clock, and went six miles. Passed the snake's den.

May 18.—Traveled about seventeen miles over the bluffs. Very little timber, but good water.

May 19.—Traveled about eighteen miles. Passed one • grave. An Indian farm about four miles west of the toll bridge kept by the Sac and Fox Indians. Toll, 25 cents. Passed one of the most beautiful pictures of country I ever saw. Drove the team with Mason.

May 20.—Traveled about sixteen miles over beautiful rolling prairie. No timber. Passed some new graves. Passed one horse and one ox left to die at leisure.

May 21.—Tuesday. Passed the grave of A. Powers, of Peoria County, Illinois, died on the 20th inst., about sixty-five miles west of St. Joseph. Traveled about eighteen miles. Was called to visit three cases of cholera. One died, a man, leaving a wife and child, from Illinois, poor. He lived seven hours after being taken. No wood or water secured.

May 22.—Rainy. Traveled five miles, and came to wood and water in plenty. Went on about ten miles further, and put out for the night. Fleming and Curtis taken with the cholera. Wake all night. Called upon just before we stopped to see a man with the cholera, who died soon after.

May 23.—Curtis and Fleming better, but not able to start in the morning. Started at 12, and traveled about six miles. Plenty of water three-quarters of a mile north of the road. Stopped in camp with Dr. Bemis's company. Heard wolves during the night.

May 24.—Started early. Curtis and Fleming pretty comfortable. Traveled about nineteen miles. Passed the forks leading to Independence. Camped at Blue river. One grave, child 11 years old. Forded the stream. Raised our loading. Got my medicines wet. Boys caught a meal of catfish. Fish were large and plenty, and included enough for tomorrow's breakfast.

May 25.—Started at Big Blue river. Took in company Samuel J. Hunter. Left the river at half past 3. Another grave.' Traveled ten miles.

May 26.—Traveled about five miles and rested. Had catfish for breakfast.

May 27.—Went in with John Childs's train of ten wagons. At night the company lacked water, having camped on a hill away from water and wood. Traveled eighteen miles. Saw an antelope.

May 28.—Late start. Traveled alone, about fifteen miles. Plenty of feed and tolerable water. Passed four graves. Camped on a dry hill, a few rods from the Childs train.

May 29.—Started at 6 o'clock, going about eighteen miles. Water scarce and poor. Curtis gave the milk away. Went without dinner. A drove of buffaloes were seen by a company ahead. Left the team and went on ahead. Saw one buffalo and one antelope. Took sick with the cholera. No one meddled or took any notice of it but George Moon.

May 30.—Feel better. Start on foot. Continue to get better. Travel up the Little Blue twenty miles. Wood, water and feed tolerable.

May 31.—Started at 6. Followed up the Blue. Passed one good spring. Feed short. Traveled twenty miles. Hunter left, and I took the cooking line.

June 1.—Left the range of the Blue. Traveled twenty miles. Saw three antelopes.

June 2.—Started late. Rode all the forenoon, and read. Traveled eleven miles. Put up on the Platte. No wood or good water.

June 3.—Started at half past 6. Traveled five miles to Fort Kearney. Saw tame buffaloes. The fort buildings are built of wood, brick and mud. The country is flat and rather low. Two miles southeast are sandhills in sight. Went about twenty-two miles, and fell in with innumerable hosts of immigrants. Rained through the night.

June 4.—Traveled up the Platte river twenty miles. The road was low, level and muddy. The river is about a mile wide. At 2 o'clock it began to rain and blow tremendously, continuing all night. Camped without a spark of fire or warm supper, with our clothes as wet as water. A man died with the cholera in sight of us. He was a Mason. 1 was called to see him, but too late.

June 5.—It rains yet. Got as wet as ever in getting the team. I got a chance to cook some meat and tea with Dr. Hotchkiss's stove. In company with Mr. Stone from

Mansfield. Have a bad headache; take a blue pill. Start at 9; travel to a creek, twelve miles.

June 6.—Start at 9. Unship our load, and cross a creek. One death, a Missourian, from cholera. Go eighteen miles. Pass four graves in one place. Two more of the same train are ready to die. Got a pint and a half of brandy. Earn $2.20. Left Krill with a dying friend.

June 7.—Start late. Find plenty of doctoring to do. Stop at noon to attend some persons sick with cholera. One was dead before I got there, and two died before the next morning. They paid me $8.75. Deceased were named Israel Broshears and William Broshears and Mrs. Morton, the last being mother to the bereaved widow of Israel Broshears. We are 85 or 90 miles west of Fort Kearney.

June 8.—Left the camp of distress on the open prairie at half past 4 in the morning. The widow was ill both in body and mind. I gave them slight encouragement by promising to return and assist them along. I overtook our company at noon twenty miles away. Went back and met the others in trouble enough. I traveled with them until night. Again overtook our company three miles ahead. Made my arrangements to be ready to shift my duds to the widow's wagon when they come up in the morning.

Israel — Catherine's husband
Mrs. Morton — Catherine's mother

June 9.—Started off in good season. Went twenty miles. Encamped on a creek. Wolves very noisy, keeping us awake all night.

June 10.—Traveled eleven miles, and crossed South Platte at the lower crossing. Stream three-fourths mile wide, with a heavy current.

June 11.—Traveled twenty-one miles. Waded for wood for self and Rider. Got small ash poles.

Here there is a break in the doctor's journal, there being no entries from June 12th to 24th inclusive. This is the only omission in the entire journey from Missouri river to Puget Sound. It is to be supposed that the troubles were so many and the labors so great incident to the peculiar situation in which he found himself that he then was unable to keep the diary written up as he did before and after the events in connection with the unfortunate Morton-Broshears party. Seven members of the party died there and then, Mrs. Broshears losing not only her husband and mother but three other relatives, and being left is a most forlorn and helpless condition. The sympathy and assistance she required from the doctor, who subsequently became her second husband, accounts reasonably for this much to be regretted omission in the narrative.

Tuesday, June 25.—Started late, in consequence of our cattle being lost. When I came in from hunting the cattle the company had gone and left us. We drove on to the Bad Hills, about eighteen mines, and encamped.

June 26.—Started from camp in tolerable season, after burying Austin Morton. Drove two miles and camped. Feed is poor, and plenty of stock to eat it. Took care of the team alone.

June 27.—George Benton commenced driving the team. Went ten miles to Cottonwood Creek; camp there and wash up. Feed is good and water excellent. I cannot persuade the company to stop half long enough to recruit the team. Parr with Fanings & Co.

June 28.—Finished our washing and took a trip to the mountain four miles south. I think this the pleasantest hunting ground I ever saw. Team came in at night full and lively.

June 29.—Left camp and traveled over to the North Platte again. Went ten miles and camped. Feed poor.

June 30.—Traveled about fourteen miles to the ferry. Crossed our teams over, leaving the oxen on the east side. Had a serious tramp in carrying supper to the boys, after dark, some six or seven miles and back.

July 1.—Brought teams to the stream to ford. After working two-thirds of the day we had nine oxen to ferry across at $1 per head. Drove out five miles and camped without feed or water.

July 2.—Traveled over rough hills about twenty miles to Willow Springs. Feed poor, water a little touched with alkali. Found plenty of saleratus water, by which our teams suffered much.

July 3.—Left Willow Springs, and traveled over barren, rough mountains about twenty miles to big creek. No feed.

July 4.—Left the big creek and went ten miles to Independence Rock. Celebrated a little. Found feed very scarce. Rider's hired hand came, and agreed to come on with him.

July 5.—Dragged the team through sand eight miles to Devil's Gate, and turned out and drove team three miles to feed. This pass through the rocks of the Whitewater is one of the curiosities of nature. Perpendicular height of rocks four hundred feet. Width of stream or valley fifty-five feet.

July 6.—Drove the team to camp and took wagons out to grass. Oxen sick; vomiting like dogs. Old Nig looks bad. Get better towards night.

July 7.—Go on a trip to the mountain. See a large panther and five antelopes. Got spruce gum and snow. Got into camp about 3 o'clock, tired enough.

July 8.—Started out, and after traveling six miles discovered a party of Indians coming upon us. We heard they had just robbed one train. Prepared for an attack. When within half a mile they sent two of their number to see how strong we were. After viewing us carefully they left us for good. Traveled twenty-two miles.

July 9.—Left the creek by spells, and traveled through the Narrows twenty miles and camped. Bought buffalo meat. Kept guard for fear of Mormons. Team comfortably fed.

July 10.—Traveled in sand all day, and camped without water or feed. Came twenty miles.

July 11.—Started before breakfast, and came eight miles to Sweetwater. Stopped, took breakfast, and went on to the Sweetwater again, camped; fourteen miles.

July 12.—Left Sweetwater and traveled over the ragged mountains twenty miles. I was well worn out, as well as the team, from watching at night. A miserable company for help.

July 13.—Left the ice spring. Team poorly fed. Traveled eight miles to the last of the Sweetwater. Turned out with a view to stopping, but the company growled, and we again set sail. Went on in search of feed and water until all power was exhausted. Team got ahead about five miles. Camped, with little feed and no water.

14

July 14.—Team tolerably fed, but no water. Traveled eight miles to Pacific Springs. Watered and filled water cask. Wrote a line to Henry (Maynard's son). Paid 50 cents to carry it to St. Joseph. I then went ahead in search of feed and water. Found some feed but no water, and got no thanks from the company for my labor.

July 15.—Left camp and passed the forks of the roads, the left road leading to Salt Lake. Traveled eight miles to the Little Sandy. Watered the team, drove three miles more, turned out and camped. Drove the team up four miles further for feed. Set things at right about camp, carried supper to the boys four miles, washed, changed clothes and slept in tent.

July 16.—Found good feed for team four and a half miles from camp, and stayed to rest our teams and wash in the waters of Little Sandy. Company growled so much I consented to start next morning. Found ice in the water bucket this morning.

July 17.—Got under way at 8, and drove twelve miles to Big Sandy. I went in search of feed; tramped about eleven miles, and found feed scarce. Returned to camp, and sent the boys out with teams to graze all night. The water of the Sandy is made of the snow melting on the mountains in sight.

July 18.—Left camp at 11 o'clock with our water vessels all filled, to cross the desert, fifty-three miles, to Green river. Traveled all day and night. Dust from one to twelve inches deep on the ground and above the top of the wagon cover a perfect cloud. Crossed a plain of twelve miles, and then went over a tremendous mountain.

July 19.—Arrived at Green river about noon. Paid $7 per wagon for ferrying. Drove out eight miles to grass on a branch of Green river. Put cattle in the brush and let them go.

July 20.—Drove the cattle out to feed. Watched them ail day myself. George caught four trout, which made us a good breakfast. Drove in the team about 10 in the evening. Lion, Sam and Bright are sick.

July 21.—Company was not willing to feed the team or for me to doctor Lion. We therefore start without even watering team. Came on about four miles and camp. Teams falling behind. Went back to learn the cause. Found them too weak to travel. Went on and left them. Travel fifteen miles to a branch of Green river.

July 22.—Left camp at 8 o'clock. Found a rough mountainous road. Traveled to the ten springs among the spruce. Feed scarce. Came Fifteen miles. Rain stopped us from going further. Rider came up at eve, drove past, and camped in sight. Got the tent in which George and I slept.

July 23.—Climbed mountains at the start. Passed Rider's team after they camped. Drove about a mile, and found good water and good feed. Went eighteen miles.

July 24.—Began climbing the mountains at 7, and went over the worst ones I ever saw teams encounter. Crossed a a branch of Green river. Passed through a beautiful grove of spruce and fir. We threw Lion down, and found four or five gravel stones in his foot. Came eighteen miles and camped, with most excellent water and feed.

July 25.—Left camp at 6:30, after throwing Lion and doctoring his foot, which Mrs. Broshears, George and myself did alone. This day the mountains have capped the climax. Crossed Bear river, and traveled down the valley. Find good water and the best of feed. The mountains present the grandest display of nature yet seen. Rocks two feet thick stand upon edge from thirty to one hundred feet high about four or six feet apart.

July 26.—Left camp at 7. Traveled down Bear river until noon. Found excellent feed. Crossed another branch and ascended a mountain about three miles, and then turned down about one mile almost perpendicularly to the river bottom again.

July 27.—Started out on the Bear river bottom. Traveled up the river a north course twenty-four miles. Passed beautiful springs and plenty of feed. Doctored Lion's foot twice. The springs as they make from the mountains form considerable streams. Indians are plenty. Saw Rider's team some three miles astern.

July 28.—Left camp at 7. Good water, feed and roads. Came fourteen miles to sulphur or soda springs. A trading post. Springs are a curiosity. Went on about a mile, and fed forenoon at an Indian camp. Was called to see a sick pappoose. Sold five pounds of tobacco for $2.50. Went on seven miles and camped near an Indian camp. Good feed and water.

July 29.—Broke camp at 7:30. Teams in good heart. Found good roads, feed and water. Traveled sixteen miles and crossed the head waters of Bear river. Shot two mountain hen, and encamped for the night at a spring. Feed first rate. We are just at the foot of a mountain to start with in the morning. Stream is too bad to cross. Doctored Lion's foot, and fed poor Bright.

July 30.—Left the waters of Bear river, and struck the waters of Louis river. Had rather a rough road, but the best of water and wood. Encamped, and was called to visit sick with the diarrhoea. He was taken sick in the night, from cold and billious condition of the stomach.

July 31.—Left camp at 7:30. Roads, feed and water tolerable. Got to Fort Hall. Took supper. Found the mosquitoes so bad that it was impossible to keep the oxen or ourselves on that spot. Hitched up and came on to the Fort and camped in the dust. Watched the cattle until morning.

August 1.—Left Fort Hall at 9. Sold rice, salt, soap to the traders; bought moccasins and one quart of vinegar. Came on, and crossed two branches of Lewis river. Traveled eighteen miles. Camped on a ridge among the sage. Oh, God! the mosquitoes. Drove team up on the bluff to rest. Took in George the Second at the Fort. Sick all day and under the influence of calomel pills.

August 2.—Found team where they were when I went to bed. Drove them down on the bottom to feed. We had veal for breakfast, presented to us by a brother Mason from New Orleans. Went eight miles through the sage to a spring, and put old Lion out to rest. Started at 2, and made out fifteen miles, and encamped for the night. Passed two springs of cold water which boiled up so high as to make them a great curiosity. Passed the American Falls on Snake river.

August 3.—Started late on Lion's account. Drove two and a half miles, and he gave up the ghost. We then harnessed Nigger on the lead, and traveled on seven and one-half miles down the. Snake river, and put out for the night in quite a hubbub. George is about to leave us for California.

19

Road is bad, full of gullies and rocks. Feed poor, sage brush all the way. Plenty of cedar shrubs along the way.

August 4.—Traveled ten miles over a rough road to Raft river, and laid up until Monday (tomorrow) morning. The boys caught a plenty of suckers. Rigged Nig's harness.

August 5.—Started late. Left the tent. Lost our water keg. Sixteen miles to water. Very warm. Took up a new bag of flour. Started at the forks of the road on the Oregon track. Road very stony. Traveled all day through the sage and dust. Encamped on a spring run with plenty of feed.

August 6.—Left camp early. Traveled eleven miles over sage and came to the river where we found plenty of feed for our cattle. Stopped three hours. Then went on to Goose Creek, eleven miles further, and camped for the night with good feed and water. Saw one wolf in the road ahead. Good roads today, and water often enough for the cattle.

August 7.—Stayed in camp and rested our team. Rider came up at night. Nigger died. Washed, etc.

August 8.—Left camp early, and found a very stony road. Traveled eighteen miles to Rocky Creek. Found poor feed for team.

August 9.—Traveled eighteen miles to the crossing of Rock creek. Got in late. Feed scarce. Were overrun with cattle and company.

August 10.—Traveled fifteen miles to where the road leaves the river bluffs. Put out and let our team graze on the bottoms until next day.

August 11.—Left early, and went over sage nine miles, coming to the river again. Then went down the bottom, occasionally raising over the bluffs, seven miles to Salmon Falls creek, then down the creek and river bottom three miles to camp. Good feed and water.

August 12.—Started at 6:30. Traveled ^ix miles to Salmon Falls. Here we camped, and bought salmon of the Indians, and refreshed our teams. This place is delightful. The stream is alive with fish of the first quality, and wild geese are about as tame as the natives. Soil continues barren.

August 13.—Left camp at 4 o'clock a m., and traveled thirteen miles to the river again. Here we encamped, laying by until tomorrow morning. Had a hard time bringing water from the river, the nearest being half a mile distant and up one of the worst of bluffs.

August 14.—Started at 5 in the morning. Climbed a hard hill of sand. Came ten miles to river, then left the river and came on to it again in three miles, where the old road crosses. Then drove down the track three miles and found a good camp, and plenty of rattlesnakes. George has been sick all day. I have driven the team and am tired enough.

August 15.—Stayed in camp, aired our clothes, etc. Killed, three rattlesnakes. Got information of the route from Government men packing from Oregon City. Watched team all night.

August 16.—Left at 6. Traveled down the river sixteen miles and camped. Found good feed, but a stony, hard road. The country is as barren as ever. Watched team all night.

August 17.—Left camp at 6. Came over bluffs, alternately touching the river, ten miles, to where we crossed Boone's river. There we stopped, and let our team graze. Feed best we have seen yet. Moving on again we came to the river in six miles, and encamped. Feed good and team doing well. Watched team all night.

August 18.—Left camp at 8. Came over the bluff and down the river eight miles, thence six miles to camp on the river bank. Feed very poor for team. Watched them all night. Am nearly sick, but no one knows it but myself.

August 19.—Left camp at 6. Traveled six miles over the bluffs to Cade's creek. No feed. Went on two miles further and came to bunch grass. At 11 o'clock stopped, and refreshed our animals until 1. Started again and came six miles to Burnt creek. ' Crossed creek and climbed the worst of all hills. Went up three times to get our load up. Took up old Brandy; overhauled wagon.

August 20.—Geared the wagon shorter. Threw overboard some of our load. Started at 7, with Brandy in Sally's place. He stood up for about three miles, when down he came, and we unyoked him and Polly and moved on with three yoke of cattle. Stopped at 11:30 and rested the team. Started at 1, and went over to the river, making 14 miles this day. Found good feed and rested self and team.

August 21.—Cut off the wagon bed and again overhauled. Started at 8, and hurried along 6y miles down the river to a spring, camping at noon. Good feed and plenty of company. Laid by and rested team. Bought salmon of Indians. Left this morning a distressed family who were without team or money and nearly sick from trouble.

August 22.—Left camp at 6. Came three miles to river, and then down same eleven miles to camp. Left Brandy and Polly to die on the road. Found feed tolerable, but water scarce as soon as we were away from the river.

August 23.—Left camp at 6, and traveled to next camp, on Snake river.

August 24.—Left camp at 7. Went six miles and turned out to water and rest our teams. Put Polly in with Bright, and left Buck. Got loaded and started at 1. Came to Auhihie (Owyhee) river. Here we found excellent feed for team, and laid up until next evening. Ducks and sage hens are very plenty.

August 25.—Laid in camp with team. I went to the fort, four miles, to get more teams, but found none there. Returned at noon. Cut off more of the wagon bed and brought the wheels closer together. Left camp at 5, and went on for sulphur springs nineteen miles ahead.

August 26.—Found ourselves this morning at 5 o'clock about nine miles from Fort Boise. Stopped and got breakfast. Found plenty of bunch grass, but no water for cattle. Stopped twice during the night and rested teams. Came about thirteen miles before we put up to rest or recruit. Plenty of feed for team, but horrible sandy roads. Fort Boise is a miserable hole, with one white man and fourteen Sandwich Island niggers.

August 27.—Found ourselves this morning on the road six miles back from Branch creek. Came on to it, and put up for the rest of the day. Here we found a place where we could stand with one foot in water hot enough for culinary purposes and the other in good, cool water to drink. Left camp at dark, for fear of Indians, and traveled until 11 o'clock, when we turned out for three hours.

August 28.—Started this morning at 2, and came on four miles to sulphur springs. Here we stopped, and breakfasted ourselves and team. Then moved on ten miles to Birch creek, at 1 o'clock. Mrs. B. drove the cattle and let me take a nap in her bed. Left Birch creek, and came three and a half miles to the river.

August 29.—Left camp at 6 in the morning, and came six miles to Burnt river. Made a yoke of an old axle. Started out again at 6 in the evening, and came five miles to a branch of Burnt river.

August 30.—Started at midnight. Came on to a branch of Burnt creek. Here we laid up and rested our team and driver until half past 3 p m., when we again started out, came four miles and camped until the moon was up, when we resumed our march.

August 31.—Started out under a favorable breeze, down hill, the team going as if the devil was at their heels, and we shot out to the Slough, eight miles, in good time. Watered and went on a mile and fed on good grass. This makes us one hundred miles since Sunday evening at Fort Boise. Came to Powder river at 9:30.

Sunday, September 1.—Started at half past 4, after being up with team nearly all night. Came on to the Good camp at spring. On our way here at Powder river we killed a noble salmon, taking breakfast out of him, and a fine dish it was. I just wish my family had such a fish to work at. From Fort Boise 114 miles. Encamped at first spring on the Grand Ronde.

September 2.—Left camp at 6-1/4. Stopped and let the team feed twice before noon. Came on to the bluffs, 7-1/2 miles, at 11. Took dinner. Saw sand hill cranes and sage hens in plenty. In the Ronde found the best grass we have seen since we left home. Here we began climbing the Blue mountains, and if they don't beat the devil. Came on eight miles to Ronde river, and camped.

September 3.—On our way at 4. Came over the mountains and through a dense forest of pine, twenty miles, to camp springs. Here we overtook Bichard and Thurman.

September 4.—Left camp early and traveled fifteen and a half miles to the foot of the mountains. Encamped among the Kiuse and Walla Walla Indians. Poor feed for cattle, as the Indian horses had eaten it off. Here we got peas and potatoes.

September 5.—Traded for a mare and colt and Indian dress, and came on ten miles. Paid for the things a brass kettle, two blankets, a shirt, etc.

September 6.—Left camp early and went twenty miles to second crossing of the Umatilla river. Here we found a very intelligent Indian. Good grass. Bought a fine spotted horse, which cost me $55.

September 7.—Stayed in camp until about dark, when we started out, going eight miles, to a place on the Umatilla river. Good grass, wood and water.

September 8.—Sunday. Came to the Columbia river, twenty miles, through the sand all the way. This night I had my horse stolen. I was taken about sunset with the dysentery, which prostrated me very much.

September g.—Started in search of my horse before it was light. Found he had been stolen. Put out and left and came down the Columbia twelve miles. Encamped alone, with good feed, wood and water.

September 10.—Left at 6, and came on seventeen miles to a creek. Feed rather scarce. I drove all day. George came up at night from hunting the horse.

September 11.—Left at 6^2. Came nineteen miles. Camped on the Columbia at the island. Feed poor, but sand plenty.

September 12.—Traveled about fifteen miles. Camped on a creek. Came up some of the worst bluffs on the road.

September 13.—Came sixteen miles, to the river five miles above the falls. Road better. No feed.

September 14.—Left early. Crossed falls of the river and came on to a creek six miles from the Dalles. Encamped for good. Came to the conclusion that the team would never stand driving over the Cascade mountains.

September 15.—Left the team at the creek. Went to the Dalles and got some flour of Government officers at 25 cents a pound, and salt pork at 12^ cents.

September 16.—Drove to the Dalles. Sold the cattle to a Mr. Wilson for $110, and prepared to start for Portland down the river. Let George have $5. Set up nearly all night and watched the goods.

September 17.—Loaded up our boat and left. Paid $17 for freight and passage. Left the wagon with Nathan Olney, to be forwarded to Portland as soon as practicable. Came down about fifteen miles and landed for the night. We

28

buried a child which we found upon the bank of the river, drowned.

September 18.—Started at daylight. Came four miles and landed for breakfast; then ran down to the Cascade falls, landed, and camped for the night.

September 19.—Hired a team and got our goods down below the rapids. Engaged Chenoweth to start out with us immediately, but he, being a scoundrel, did not do as he agreed, and we were obliged to stay until next morning.

September 20.—Hired an Indian to carry us down in his canoe to Fort Vancouver. We had a hard time, in consequence of the Indian being so damned lazy. By rowing all the way myself we got to the fort at 1 in the morning as wet as the devil.

September 21.—Got a room and put up our things to dry. Found a gentleman in the person of Mr. Brooks.

September 22.—Left the fort with two Indians, who took us down the Columbia thirty-eight miles to the mouth of the Cowalitz and up the Cowalitz two miles to Judge Burbee's, in good season. Here we were kindly received, and treated as if old acquaintances.

September 23.—Left the Judge's, loaded with kindness, and under pole came up the Cowalitz, which is a very hard

29

stream to ascend. Encamped for the night under the protecting shade of lofty fir and hemlock trees. Slept very little.

September 24.—Set sail again under an ash breeze, and came to Plomondon's landing about noon. Obtained horses and started out ten miles to Mr. J. R. Jackson's, where we were received very kindly and kept free over night.

September 25.—With an early start, made our way twenty miles to Mr. S. S. Ford's for dinner. From this we made our way through dense forest and uneven plain twenty-five miles to M. T. Simmons's, our place of destination, where we were received with that degree of brotherly kindness which seemed to rest our weary limbs, and promise an asylum for us in our worn-out pilgrimage.

The journey across the continent was a hard one to all. There was constant struggle and suffering; fear of Indians, Mormons, deep and turbulent rivers, mountain climbings and starvation; worry unceasing concerning the animals and vehicles of the train, and of the wandering and helpless members of the family; uncertainty as to the future, that at times became distressing; dirt everywhere, sickness and disease, and frequently death. The immigrants tired of themselves and tired of each other. Stretching out these unhappy conditions for a period of four or five months, as but faintly portrayed in diaries such as the foregoing, drove some of the participants into suicide, others into insanity, and left many a physical wreck for whom there was no possibility of recovery. Even the stoutest of mind and body, combining usually the best natures in the party, were so worn and exhausted by the end of the trip that they could no longer restrain their exhibitions and exclamations of impatience, of irritation, and of complaint. Doctor Maynard was one of this class. No one ever crossed the plains better equipped mentally and physically than he, more helpful and self reliant, more able to lead and direct, more prepared for wise action in any emergency or contingency that might occur. He was one of the most jovial of men, whose good humor could hardly be disturbed, and who was always smoothing out troubles, doing personal favors and calming the agitations of those about him. And yet even he could not continue to the end without showing some signs of the ill feelings he experienced. The entries in his diary the last few days are referred to, and particularly the one relating to Chenoweth. Chenoweth was not a scoundrel by any means. He was a young lawyer, who had settled at the Cascades, where he was endeavoring to practise his profession, and at the same time conduct a hotel and carry people and merchandise by sail vessel to and from the settlements on the lower Columbia and Willamette rivers. Five years later he was one of the three United States judges for the Territory of Washington; during which time Maynard served under him as clerk and commissioner, when they became intimate and excellent friends. Afterwards he went to Oregon, where he died, after a long, useful and honorable career.

TRIPS TO SOUTH AND NORTH

DR. MAYNARD began at once to acquaint himself with the new country to which he had undesignedly come. Before establishing himself he concluded to look at Portland, Oregon City and the country in their vicinity. Of the trip one way he made the brief notes following:

Tuesday, Oct. 8.—Left M. Simmons's on horseback for the Wallamet [Willamette River] on an excursion. Came to S. S. Ford's. Met with friend visiting the valley of the Sound. Stayed overnight with them.

Oct. 9.—Came on to Jackson's, took dinner and then to Warbass's. Engaged our Indians to take us over to the Wallamet. Stopped overnight.

Oct. 10.—Left early, and came down to Tebo's, and stopped overnight.

Oct. 11.—Put out and came up the' Columbia to Deer island, stopping for the night at Mr. Merrill's.

Oct. 12.—Came on to the mouth of the Wallamet, and stopped at Mr. Miller's for the night.

The record is cut off here. The Doctor undoubtedly reached Portland the next day, being six days in making a trip that can now be made in six hours.

Upon his return to Olympia Maynard resolved next time to go north. A government geologist named Evans had recently reported coal on Steilaguamish river. Samuel Hancock claimed to know of it, too. Major H. A. Goldsborough, who had been on the Sound a few months, also had some knowledge of it, which he imparted freely. About the same time Patkanim, chief of the Snoqualmie Indians, then a strong but troublesome tribe, came upon the scene. Maynard employed him in the making of the trip and for the purpose of the discovery which he contemplated. They started together November 18th, with six Indians to move the canoe and do the work. The Doctor's account of the trip is as follows:

Monday, Nov. 18.—Left Olympia, and went down the Sound eight miles, and encamped under a slab house of our own building. Saw Simmons and Judge Strong at Round Point. Rain.

Nov. 19.—Left camp early, and traveled about twenty miles, to the entrance of the [Tacoma] Narrows. Encamped. Rain.

Nov. 20.—Left camp and sailed a part of the way in the rain. Stopped, and bought salmon and potatoes and mats. Camped on the beach, but were driven off before daylight by the tide. Got my gun wet. Left the skillet cover.

Nov. 21.—Left camp late, in the rain, under sail, with a stiff breeze, and ran around to an Indian camp, where we were obliged to stay until next morning for the wind.

Nov. 22.—Left camp early, and ran into the mouth of the Snohomish a short distance and encamped. Found the banks low and marshy, with little timber.

Nov. 23.—Started early and traveled against tide and current about twelve miles. Met with a nest of Indians. Stopped, and had a long chat with them, but learned nothing of use to our object.

Nov. 26.—Paid for canoe one blanket, two shirts, three looking glasses and other iktas to the amount of 62 cents.

Unfortunately the entries of Nov. 24th and 25th and 27th and 28th have been torn from the book, so that all that is known of the trip in the Doctor's own handwriting is that contained in the foregoing. It is known from other sources, however, that coal was discovered, and that Maynard sold his information and rights to Sargent, upon his return to Olympia. Evidently the coal was not much, tho, as in all the years since it has remained undeveloped. Dr. Maynard was suspicious of Patkanim, and watched him closely during the entire trip. The year before an attack had been made by the Snoqualmies upon Fort Nisqually, and two white men killed, for which Patkanim was supposed to be responsible, and for which two of the members of his band were

35

subsequently hung. He was also accused of inciting other tribes, in 1848, to a general massacre of the whites, in which effort he was unsuccessful, probably on account of the feeling of distrust with which he was generally regarded by all who knew him, Indians as well as whites. On this particular trip, tho, he apparently served his employer faithfully and well.

One of the entries in this little book is as follows:
Sold to Dr. Maynard Nov. 12th, 1850.
One bottle sweet spirits nitre $1.
Three bottles Haarlem oil $1.
One box blue mass $.50
Received payment for H. M. Knighton.
JOSEPH W. TRUTCH.

Knighton was one of the Oregon immigrants of 1845, who for a time was quite prominent. His children—three daughters and one son—have lived in Seattle for many years, the ladies being Mrs. Struve, Mrs. Parker and Mrs. Harrington. Trutch was an Englishman, acting at the time as salesman in Knighton's store. He subsequently became an engineer of distinction, was a member of British Columbia's last colonial cabinet, and was its first Lieutenant Governor, in 1871, when it became one of the Provinces of the Dominion of Canada.

December 30th, 1850, in making a trip to Fort Nisqually, Maynard notes in his diary the commission to buy of "Dr. Tolmie stovepipe and one dozen pairs of woollen socks for Simmons & Smith."

While there are many other entries in the little book they are disconnected and of varied, character, as tables of distances, lists of addresses, receipts for moneys, names of Indians, bills of goods, etc., the dates very evidently being of other times than those printed in the places where the entries are found.

A CARGO OF CORD WOOD; THE FIRST CONVENTION

ON making these trips and otherwise, Maynard had used all his small means. He had picked up a few dollars on the road, received a hundred dollars for helping the widow. Broshears from Fort Kearney to Olympia, and had also gathered in some fees for services since his arrival in September. He had lost $55 by the stealing of his horse, probably taken by the Indian from whom he bought it. Urgent necessity stared him boldly and harshly in the face. Undaunted, he took off his fine coat, donned the garments of a laborer, and proceeded to cut cord wood for the San Francisco market. He kept at it until late in the summer, when he had four hundred cords piled up on the beach in the lower part of Olympia. About this time the brig Franklin Adams, Capt. Leonard M. Felker, came seeking a load, which Maynard's woodpile furnished, the Doctor going down the coast with the vessel for the purpose of selling the cargo.

Before going, however, Dr. Maynard actively interested himself in the movement to secure the creation of a new Territory, by division of Oregon, the Columbia river being the line of separation in view. July 4th, 1851, at the celebration in Olympia of the national holiday, the suggestion was made by Col. J. B. Chapman of the future State of Columbia. It fired the patriotism of Simmons, Poe, Crosby, Maynard, Ebey, Goldsborough, Brownfield and

38

others, so that a call was at once made for the holding of a convention to take the first steps to secure what they considered the most desirable of all things—a new Territorial government. The convention assembled at Cowlitz, August 29th, and was attended by the men named and eighteen others. For two days they were in session, the results being movements ■ inaugurated for the creation of four new counties north of the Columbia river and of the new Territory. Dr. Maynard favored a State government, and a resolution presented by him called for a second convention to be held at Olympia in May, 1852, "for the formation of a State Constitution, preparatory to asking admission into the Union as one of the States." The resolution was adopted by vote of all, but the convention was not held.

IN CALIFORNIA IN 1851

AFTER selling his wood in San Francisco Maynard went to one of the gold mining districts to see his old Ohio friend, John B. Weller, who after three terms in Congress, from 1839 to 1845, d service as colonel in the Mexican war, had settled in California, and was then beginning there a career of success honorable to him in the extreme, and which included a term in the United States Senate, a term as Governor, and appointment as Minister to Mexico. Weller pointed to a chest of gold in his tent, and said: "Maynard, if you lift that off the ground I'll give half of it to you." Though a stout man, it was too heavy for the Doctor. Weller wanted Maynard to stay in California, but the latter would not, as conditions there did not suit him. During his short visit five men were killed in the camp in a foolish, wretched row, and several others lost their lives on other occasions. It was too much like a continued battle to please the peaceable physician. There was another reason, too, for Maynard's refusal. He had become interested in the widow Bro- shears, and her presence on Puget Sound was a magnet which he was unable to resist. When Weller found that Maynard was determined to return to the north, he said to him: "Doctor, let me advise you. You have the timber up there that we want and must have. Give up your profession. Get machinery and start a sawmill. In selling us lumber you'll make a hundred dollars for every one that you may possibly make in doctoring, and you'll soon be rich." He also informed him that two other former Ohioans, Henry L. Yesler and John Stroble, were then arranging to start a mill at some point not yet determined in Oregon. When Maynard platted his town of Seattle something more than a year later he named one of the streets after his friend, then U. S. Senator Weller.

RETURNS TO PUGET SOUND

UPON Dr. Maynard's return to the city he bought at auction a lot of goods that had come around the Horn by ship and were said to be damaged. They consisted of brooms, boots, molasses and such articles. He cleaned them up, and they sold as well as the best in the market. He bought more goods, and chartered Capt. Felker's vessel to carry them to Olympia. On the way up they called in at Neah Bay, where they found a British ship in distress— wrecked, in fact. The Indians had taken advantage of the unfortunate plight of the vessel and people to plunder them.

The coming in of the American brig with a small brass howitzer on board changed matters. The Indians were intimidated, and compelled under threat of bombardment to give up the stolen goods. Passengers and crew of the British ship were taken to Fort Victoria, where the rescuers were generously compensated and rewarded by the authorities. Maynard opened his goods to the public at Olympia. Several small stores were there then. He found them selling brooms at $i apiece, $i a yard for calico, $i a pound for white sugar, 50 cents a yard for domestic, and like prices generally for their goods. He cut rates for the articles named, one-half for the brooms and domestic, and three-fourths for the sugar and calico. Of course, this made a violent disturbance in trade, and the other dealers in turn

Not enough people to Dr. So he opens a store.

Chief Seattle show Maynard
Elliot Bay

made it as unpleasant for Maynard as they could. In the end they got rid of him, with the help of the great chief of the middle Sound Indians—Seattle. Seattle told Maynard that he knew a better place than Olympia for him. At this place was a harbor that would permit ships to enter at any time and get close to shore. There was a river, and near by a lake, while not far off was a road over the mountains. The soil was good, there was great hunting, and the fishing was the very best. More Indians were in that neighborhood than anywhere else, and they would work for him, trade with him and make him rich. Maynard was utterly fearless, as far as Indians were concerned. He had wonderful influence over them; his profession, as "a medicine man" having effect no doubt, in addition to which he treated them in the fairest, most honorable manner on all occasions. They believed him and trusted him. When Chief Seattle had convinced him, and offered to personally direct him to the spot, Maynard accepted the offers of lands and privileges made by the chief, who exercised sovereignty over much of the country, and immediately got ready to go to the lower Sound in the new quest for fortune and fame. Selling off such goods as he could there, he put the remainder in a large boat, and, accompanied by the Indian chief and retinue, set sail on the 27th of March, 1852.

43

He and Catherine arrive as newlyweds

LOCATES ON DUWAMISH BAY

FOUR days later they were at Alki Point [today an extremely popular Seattle beach], where a settlement had been made the previous fall by John N. Low, Charles C. Terry, Lee Terry, David T. Denny, A. Denny, Carson D. Boren and Wm. N. Bell, four of the men named having families. Maynard found that a condition of change was then imminent. Low and the Terrys intended staying at Alki. The other four men were preparing to move over to the locality Seattle was recommending to Maynard. They had examined the bay—known sometimes as Elliott and sometimes as Duwamish—during the winter, and had found it good, and as they believed, much better than the exposed roadway at Alki. The land on the east side of the bay they preferred to that on the west. They had decided among themselves as to the arrangement of their claims, but no final action had yet been taken. When Maynard arrived and announced his plans the other men were pleased. They wanted a doctor near by, and a store. Another man of his apparent energy and experience was also desirable. They urged him to settle with them. Upon looking over the ground and finding things so pleasant and promising, Maynard concluded that this was the place he was seeking, and that he would join the others in founding and establishing the proposed new settlement. He selected for his claim the land south of theirs, bounded on the north by the present Yesler Way, and extending back from the

44

bay in a compact form so as to include all that he would be entitled to under the terms of the recently-enacted donation law. For the purpose of his official land entry he named the 3d of April, 1852, as the day of his settlement. He lost no time in dreaming and scheming. Hiring white men and Indians to help him, within a week he had the house finished, and was living in it and selling goods. The building was about eighteen feet wide and twenty-six feet long, the front half having an attic and the rear but a single floor, a sort of shed attachment. Of course, it was built of logs cut on the ground near by. It stood at the present northwest corner of First avenue south and Main street, extending into the avenue, facing the tall timber on the east, and close to the water of Puget Sound on the west. In those days tide water came to First avenue in a number of places, a fact that in these later days it is difficult for newcomers to comprehend. Maynard's goods included drugs as well as groceries, tools and clothing, and his was the first mercantile effort in what is now the city of Seattle. It is only fair to say, tho, that C. C. Terry had brought a stock of merchandise to Alki Point the previous November, where he had since been conducting a store in conjunction with John N. Low, they calling their place New York, and their store the New York Mahkoke House.

45

FISH, LUMBER, LAND AND TAXES

ONE of Dr. Maynard's objects in undertaking this settlement was to put up Puget Sound fish for the San Francisco market. He had hardly got his store opened before he was employing white men in making barrels, and Indians in catching salmon. In September he had fifty Indians fishing for him. He put up nine hundred barrels of salmon that summer and fall. Piled upon the beach they made rather an imposing appearance. Later six hundred barrels were taken away by Capt. Felker on his vessel, and three hundred barrels by Capt. George Plummer. Much of the fish spoiled, no money was made, and Maynard did not repeat the effort. He also was impressed with what Senator Weller had told him about lumber, and in following the advice then received he with others loaded the brig Franklin Adams with 12,000 feet of square timber, 8,000 lineal feet of piles, 30 cords of wood and 10,000 shingles. About this time—the fall of 1852—Henry L. Yesler came along with machinery for a small sawmill. The land proprietors were all eager to get him to locate among them. The idea of a town was now entertained, and a mill employing men and inducing ships to come would be desirable to that end. To enable Yesler to get to the bay, where his mill should be built—the present northwest corner of First avenue and Yesler way—the lines of the land claims there were readjusted and a long narrow strip given him reaching far to the east. The first real estate transaction in King County was a relinquishment by David S. Maynard in favor of Yesler of the north 120 feet of Maynard's claim. This was dated the 2d of January, 1853, a few days after the legislative creation of King County, but before its formal organization. It was yet, in fact, Thurston County, with seat at Olympia, in Oregon Territory. In illustration of the newness of the country at that time, of the method of conducting official business, and of the extent of Thurston County, which then included all of Puget Sound, the advertisement following is copied from the Columbian, the first paper published on the Pacific coast north of Columbia river:

NOTICE TO TAXPAYERS.

The undersigned, collector of taxes, will be at New York and vicinity on or about the 5th of October; at Whidby Island on or about the nth; at New Dungeness on or about the 16th; at Port Townsend on or about the 20th. This notice is given for the accommodation of taxpayers so that they may be ready to pay their taxes.

A. J. SIMMONS, Sheriff.

By A. Benton Moses, Deputy and Collector of Taxes.

Though Seattle was not of sufficient consequence for the tax collector to give it a call, New York being the more important place in his estimation, it was a growing one. New people were coming, and small, cheap houses were

building for them, in most cases on Maynard's claim.
Among others was a lawyer named George N. McConaha,
with family, and about the same time or soon after came
Henry A Smith, Wm. P. Smith, E. M. Smithers, Dexter
Horton, Thomas Mercer, Edward Hanford, John C.
Holgate, Wm. A. Strickler, Chas. Plummer, R. J. Wright,
Joseph Foster, Henry Adams, Eli B. Maple, Francis
McNatt, Sidney B. Simons, John Stroble, George F. Frye,
W. G. Latimer, David Maurer, Edmund Carr, John J. Moss,
S. W. Russell, Franklin Matthias, Hillory Butler and others,
a fair proportion of them with wives and children, some of
whom settled in the incipient town, and some on land
claims near by. Most of them fimnd employment in the •
Yesler sawmill, and at times worked in the woods getting
out piles, square timbers and sawlogs. Up the Duwamish
were Luther M. Collins, Henry Van Asselt, Jacob Maple
and Samuel Maple, who had there located donation claims
in September, 1851, and who were drawing to their
neighborhood other men and families in quest of fertile
lands such as that valley afforded. In addition to these were
the Alki Pointers, or New Yorkers—Low, Terry, Renton, the
Russells, et al.—and a few others making the first
settlements in what is now Kitsap County. So much
progress was evidenced as early as the summer of 1852 that
the Commissioners of Thurston County, Oregon, on the 6th
of July established School District No. 5, the same limits
being made to include Dewamps (or Duwamish) election
precinct, created simultaneously. Within this district and

48

precinct were all of the eastern shore of Puget Sound north of Puyallup river. David S. Maynard was named as Justice of the Peace. The following December the first election was held, when A. A. Denny received all of the Dewamps votes for member of the Oregon Legislature, and was elected. It is not surprising that the ambitious men who were here getting together in a new country and new communities should be strongly affected by the agitation begun in the second half of 1852 in favor of a Territory apart from Oregon south of the Columbia. It was very inconvenient to them to go to Oregon City or Salem to enter government land or secure legislation, and the sympathies of the people there, they believed, ran more among themselves than in the direction of their distant, scattered and comparatively few fellow citizens of the north. Whether this supposition was based upon truth or not makes no difference now, but it did then, and it had weight in influencing the people in their action at that time. They were fully imbued with the American principle of self government, and to them it was much more like self government to live in and control a Territory of thirty or forty thousand square miles than it was to be an insignificant, uninfluential, out-of-the-way settlement in a Territory of ten times that area. Therefore, when the call was issued for a convention to be held at Monticello, to take steps looking to the creation of another Territory, the response was quick and glad, and nowhere more so than at the New York, Duwamish river and Seattle settlements. Of the forty-four members of that historic

49

body eight were from them, namely: John N. Low, Chas. C. Terry, Luther M. Collins, George N. McConaha, David S. Maynard, R. J. White, Wm. N. Bell and Arthur A. Denny. To these men such a trip was a serious matter, meaning at the least two weeks of time, considerable expense, much discomfort and some risk. None of them shrank or hesitated on this account.

Dr. Maynard had in view a number of matters, of personal and public interest, to induce him to attend the convention and go on to Salem, the capital. One of them was a divorce. He had long contemplated this action, but for various reasons had shrunk from its taking. He could have obtained the separation through the court at Olympia, but he did not care to make a charge against his wife or justify his own course of conduct. In the Legislature this would be unnecessary. As is usually the case with men in such affairs he thought the less that was said the better. This was without regard to the right or wrong of the matter, the justice or the injustice. It was with him as with hundreds and thousands of other pioneers—the 49ers of California as well as the early Oregonians. Men came to the Pacific coast for the purpose of getting away from unhappy family conditions, for the making of new starts in life, for their own betterment and the betterment of the world. What would have occurred at home had they not come cannot be told. It is just as well to be charitable in looking at these things. Several of the King County pioneers were in this respect as grievous offenders as Maynard, and if the facts. were all known would probably be thought much more so. Before starting the Doctor arranged his affairs as well as he could, leaving a man in charge of his business and property, and a little after the middle of the month left for Olympia, Monticello and Salem. His object at the first named place may be readily inferred. It was, of course, to see the widow Broshears. The convention met November 26th and 27th. McConaha was made president and White secretary. Upon motion of Quincy A. Brooks, a committee of thirteen members was appointed to prepare a memorial to Congress, setting forth, the situation and the desires of the people. The only two members of the convention now known to be living are Mr. Brooks and Edward J. Allen, both of whom were on this important committee. Another member of the committee was Maynard. A strong, terse, clear and comprehensive paper was formulated, the dignified and unobjectionable language of which could give no offense in the southern part of the Territory. The memorial respectfully requested of Congress the creation of the Territory of Columbia, the lands to be included being all that part of Oregon north and west of the Columbia river. The Oregon Legislature and Delegate Lane were asked to give their aid to the movement thus inaugurated. Maynard went on to Salem. There, with the assistance of Chenoweth and Ebey, the subject was presented to the Legislature, which gracefully complied with the convention's request, adopting and forwarding a short memorial upon the line indicated. The Legislature was in session during December and January. Maynard had his divorce bill introduced. It was common in the Territorial Legislatures to enact such measures prior to 1860. Sometimes twenty or more divorces were • granted. Representative Ebey opposed Maynard's application, not, however, on personal grounds, but on principle; he alleging, also, that Legislative divorces were of doubtful validity. His opposition was futile. A number of divorces were granted, as usual, Maynard's among them. Maynard urged the creation of new counties in the Puget Sound region. Bills were introduced for four such. One of them was for the county of Buchanan. The name was afterwards changed to King, the other counties being Island, Jefferson and Pierce. Pierce and King were named in honor of the two men elected the month before (November, 1852), President and Vice President of the United States. In the King County bill Maynard secured a provision locating the county seat upon his donation claim, and another fixing his house as the place for the holding of the next election. In still another bill passed while he was there, a notary public was named for each of the new counties, Maynard being the notary for King County. It is plain from the results that the Doctor was looked upon at Salem as a pretty good fellow. That he could have anything he chose to ask for that the Legislators could give was quite evident.

MARRIAGES; YESLER'S MILL; FIRST BURIAL GROUND

HIS work at the Territorial capital being accomplished, Maynard hurried back to Puget Sound. Of course, there was another stop at Olympia, where the last of the opposition to him was overcome. A few days were spent in Seattle, and then at a farmhouse in the country three or four miles back of Olympia, on the 15th of January, 1853, he and Mrs. Catherine T. Broshears were married. There was no bridal tour and no more time wasted. He had been away from home so much that he must get back to look after his interests and business. Other people wanted to get married, too, and, as there was no clergyman in Seattle and he was the local Judge, he had to hurry along. On the evening of the 23d of January, 1853, Justice Maynard united in matrimony the first white couple in Seattle, H. L. Yesler, the justice's clerk, being the witness. The ceremony was at the home of Arthur A. Denny, and the couple wedded were his brother, David T. Denny, and Mrs. Denny's sister, Louisa Boren, sister also of Carson D. Boren. This marriage turned out happily enough, as the couple lived together fifty years, and until the death of Mr. Denny, one of the most respected and honored men of the community. Another of Justice Maynard's early marriages did not result so pleasantly, the bride being Lizzie, or Betsey, a daughter of Angeline, and granddaughter of Seattle, and the groom a French scalawag named Foster, who so ill-treated her that she hung herself. Justice

Maynard had other kinds of business to attend to, of course. The first prosecutions and trials were before him. Number one was the investigation of a charge against the mate of the brig Franklin Adams of misappropriating the moneys and goods of the vessel. It was tried in Yesler's famous cookhouse. The Justice found the charge proven, but he let the mate off with admonitions never to do the like again, and thereafter to keep his accounts in better order so as to avoid repetition of like mistakes.

About this time Yesler got his mill ready to run. Maynard wanted to clear his land, so that his town lots could be seen and sold. He took a contract to supply the first logs, which he had cut by Hillory Butler and Wm. H. Gilliam from "the Point"—the land south of Main street on either side of First avenue south. This part of Maynard's claim was an island of six or eight acres in extent, the water from the Sound flowing in and out between Yesler way and Washington street on the west and at the present railroad depots on the east. The debris from the sawmill soon closed up the west opening, but that on the east admitted a gradually diminishing quantity of sea water twenty-five years longer. By the filling in process that has been so long going on on the tide lands, all trace of "the Point" has been lost. Yesler paid $7 a thousand feet for the logs, and that the price was not a big one will be apparent when it is stated that the work was all done by hand, there being neither horse nor ox employed in their moving from the stump to the bay

54

and mill. The rough lumber sold readily in San Francisco at $35 a thousand, the at times the prices paid in that city were considerably higher.

There being no public cemetery Dr. Maynard permitted a number of interments to be made on a block of his east of the Union Pacific's present depot grounds. Among these was the body of Dr. Cherry, who was killed by the Whidbey Island Indians early in 1854. He had gone there with Sheriff Russell and two other men to arrest the murderer of a man named Young, when they were fired upon and all four of the men shot, Cherry fatally. H. O. Keith, a merchant, here for his health, died of paralysis, and was there buried. George Seattle, a brother of Angeline, and a Mrs. Jemson were also laid there. The bodies of these people were never knowingly disturbed, and are there yet unless in the operations of graders they have been encountered and scattered.

PLATTING AND NAMING THE TOWN

WHEN the people first came to Seattle they found it possessed of a number of names. Parts of the land are said to have borne the Indian names Mukmukum and Tsehalalitch. The bay was called Elliott by Capt. Chas. Wilkes in 1841. Later Capt. James Alden called it Duwamish; the river, Duwamish; the point of land opposite, Duwamish Head; and the lake to the east, Duwamish lake. The authorities of Thurston County called the first election precinct Dewamps, or Duwamish. The people were not satisfied with these names. They had the absolute control of their town name, of course, and after brief deliberation they united in terming it Seattle, after the chief of the neighboring Indians. (It may be said here that then there was no Sealth known, nor until long after the death of the chief, and that his family have never recognized that name as in anywise connected with them or their ancestors.) The permission of the chief was not sought; he never showed elation at the honor paid him, nor offered objection. He was an old, dignified man, much concerned in the welfare of his people, and always on terms of warm friendship with the whites, by whom he was credited with many services of value to them during the earlier years of their settlement. The name was euphonious. Like the chief who bore it, it was popular. And so, by common consent and without dissent, the town became Seattle. It legally became the town of Seattle on the

23d of May, 1853, when David S. Maynard individually filed a plat and Carson D. Boren and Arthur A. Denny unitedly filed another plat of adjoining parts of their three claims, they' each so calling the place they were then engaged in planning and preparing for. Maynard's plat was much the larger of the two, their including twelve blocks while his included fifty-eight. His land was laid off with reference to the cardinal points; their with reference to the shore line. The map herewith pictures his plat. The names of some of the streets have been changed since by the city council. The names Jackson, King, Lane and Weller are indications of Maynard's Democratic politics. More than twenty years after his death the city government did him the honor of changing the name of a street in his donation claim and in his plat to Maynard avenue. In Maynard's plat provision was made for a public square, about a block and a half, parts of blocks 29, 30, 31 and 32, but in some way^ his intended act of generosity failed of fruition, and the public square, after his death, was turned into town lots by other men and sold. So also there was failure of another gift or attempted gift of his. On the 25th of July, 1853, he tendered to the Methodist Episcopal church a tract of land 44 rods wide by 106 rods long on the hillside east of his town site. His object was to secure there a school to be called the Seattle Institute, conducted by the church. The same day the tender was accepted as far as was then possible by the Presiding Elder, who appointed Messrs. A. A. Denny, Edmund Carr, R. H. Lansdale, George

57

Hughbanks and Wm. E. Morse a Board of Trustees for the purpose of carrying out the idea of the donor. As no subsequent action was taken the land reverted to Maynard. If the church owned this land now, so generously offered it, it would be wealthy, indeed. The first recorded sales of real estate in King County were made by D. S. Maynard. May 16th he sold to Capt. Leonard M. Felker lots 3 and 6 in block 2 for $100. Lot 6 was an inside lot alongside the present day New England Hotel, and lot 3 was in the bay immediately to the west. This was a week before the plat was filed, and several months before a lot was sold by any one else. From the beginning he sold or gave away his lots rapidly, his patrons or friends being Henry Adams, Franklin Matthias, Henry Webber, Thomas W. Slater, R. P. Willis, Charles Plummer, John A. Chase, Walter Abbott, George Plummer, David Maurer, John J. Moss, Solomon Collins, L. V. WyckoffW. P. Smith, L. M. Felker and others in Seattle, and to prominent men of the Territory elsewhere, as Elwood Evans, Wm. H. Wallace, Daniel S. Howard, J. Patton Anderson, J. S. Clendenin, Chas. H. Mason, W. W. Miller, Hugh A. Goldsborough and James Tilton. He received for his lots $1, $5, $10, $20, $25, $50 and in one case $100, lots that today are worth from $50,000 to $100,000 apiece. His largest sale at this time was to Capt. Felker, the block bounded now by Jackson and King streets, First avenue south and Railroad avenue— the so-called Point—for $350. Felker built a fine house upon it, at an expense of $4,000, in which court was held, and which was a favorite boarding house until its destruction by fire June 6th, 1889. Felker sold the block and house to A. C. Anderson in 1861 for $2,000, and Anderson about thirty years later sold the land for $51,000. Block 52 Dr. Maynard deeded to four of his Eastern relatives, including his son and daughter. He paid the taxes upon it while living, but after his death the taxes were allowed to go unpaid, and the block was sold by the county to Melody Choir. In consequence of his enterprise, generosity and prodigality Maynard's lots went quickly. He would sell for almost any price that he could obtain. As a result the town was upon his claim during the first years of its existence, and it was not until in the 80's that the business center crossed Yesler way. Having disposed of his land, however, the increased values given to it by the people and business he induced to locate upon it did not help him. In this respect—the one of personal benefit to himself and wife—his course was not so prudent as that adopted by Yesler, Denny, Terry and other large property owners, who, while encouraging the coming of new people, did not rob themselves for their good, but rather shared with them the advantages to be derived from the increase of population and business and growth of the town.

Dr. Maynard's character may be illustrated by an anecdote. He was prepared to turn his hand to anything useful. His experience on the Plains had not only made a teamster of him, but he thought a blacksmith. No one else offering to open a shop in his town, Maynard in the summer of 1853 purchased and installed a bellows, anvil, tools and materials on lot one of block seven, the southeast corner of First avenue south and Washington street. There he shod the draft animals of the Duwamish farmers. In town there was neither horse nor ox. While so engaged on the 1st of September, one of the newcomers—a tall, powerful, young man, named Lewis V. Wyckoff—stopped and remarked to him:

"You are doing pretty well for a doctor, but it is plain you never served time as a blacksmith's apprentice."

"I never did; that's true," replied the physician, "and I'm not doing this because I like it. But, maybe, you think you have served time."

"Yes, I have; and I'm a good blacksmith, too," said Wyckoff.

"Perhaps, then, you'd like to own this shop?"

"I would like to have it, but I haven't the money with which to buy it," said Wyckoff, thinking that Maynard was likely to ask a big price.

"Well, if you want it, and will promise to run it," Maynard remarked, "you can have it cheap enough, and on terms to suit you."

"Name your price, Doctor," the sturdy blacksmith said.

"If you will keep the shop open, and do the people's work, I'll give you the entire outfit, and sell you the lot for ten dollars."

"They're mine," shouted the astonished Wyckoff. "Here's your money. Give me the deed."

Before night the quit claim deed from Maynard to Wyckoff was on file at the auditor's office. Probably no man in Seattle had more varied and diverse employments than D. S. Maynard. Anything good enough for other men to do was good enough for him—if useful, desirable, or profitable—and what he did he usually did well. The story also exemplifies his liberality or reckless open-handedness.

Seattle's First Courts and Their Business he Territory of Washington having been created by Congress in March, 1853, and Gov. Stevens having proclaimed its organization in November following by establishment of election precincts and appointment of officers, and the formation of the Legislative and Judicial districts, the calling of an election and so forth, special progress was made by Seattle in consequence. It was one of the two precincts of the county, the other one being Alki. H. L. Yesler, A. A. Denny and D. S. Maynard were appointed by the Governor as the officers of election, which was held on the 30th of January, 1854. King was made a Representative district by itself, but was joined with Pierce in the Council district. All of Puget Sound north of Thurston County was constituted the Third Judicial District, with terms of court at Steilacoom, Seattle, Coveland and Port Townsend. The term of court ordered by the Governor to be held at Seattle in February was found to be impossible. The first' term, therefore, was in October, 1854, Chief Justice Lander presiding. Thomas S. Russell was Sheriff; David S. Maynard, Clerk; Frank Clark, Prosecuting Attorney for the Territory, and El wood Evans Attorney for the United States by special appointment. The first complaints were against Captains Rand, Pray, Newell and Collins, for discharging ballast in the Sound. The charges were held against these mariners until the next term of Court, when they were dismissed by Judge Chenoweth, probably because of the newness of things, lack of knowledge of law and the custom in the past for shipmasters to dump "ballast at pleasure. The next man brought in for that offense, however, was not let off so easily; Capt. Marshall Blinn, in April, 1855, being convicted and fined. At the first term of Court the Grand Jury consisted of Chas. C. Terry, Wm. N. Bell, S. M. Holderness, O. M. Eaton, Francis McNatt, Edmund Carr, Franklin Matthias, Henry VanAsselt, Wm. H. Gilliam, Henry Pierce, C. C. Lewis, B. L. Johns, Abram F. Bryant, Joseph Foster, William Heebner, G. W. W. Loomis, Wm. P. Smith, H. H. Tobin, J. L. Foster and Burley Pierce. In 1853 Mesatchee Jim, a bad Indian, as indicated by his name, had killed his wife without cause or reason. The white men did not like

62

Jim or his act, and a party of them, organized for the purpose, promptly seized him and hung him in the outskirts of town. The attention of the Grand Jury was called to this act of lawlessness by Judge Lander and Prosecutor Clark, the result being the indictment of David Maurer for murder, October 24th. On the 26th the Jury filed into Court, and after a statement to the Judge by Foreman Terry, Loomis and Heebner were dismissed. Heebner was one of the leading actors in the lynching, and while that fact did not seem to militate against him as a juror in the indictment of Maurer, it hardly seemed to be the proper thing for him to assist in his own indictment. The jury retired and immediately indicted Heebner for murder. Later Luther M. Collins was added to the prisoners so accused. Robert Brainard was similarly indicted, but Loomis escaped. Maurer was tried first. He was a simple-minded Dutchman. When the plain statement in the indictment was read to him in Court, and he was asked by the Judge whether he was guilty or not, he was frightened, and hesitated and stammered, according to Butler, Yesler, Foster and others of the pioneers then present. "Vat ish de question, Shudge?" he is said to have asked. It was read to him again, when he innocently replied, "I suppose I ish quilty, Shudge." Terry is said to have leaned over and whispered to him, "Not guilty, you fool, say not guilty," whereupon Maurer amended his plea by saying "not guilty." The first admission was disregarded by the Court and the declaration of innocence was entered

63

on the record instead. Maurer cried with fear, thinking he would be hung, saying he would never see his family again, and he felt so bad. The trial jurors were Henry H. Decker, Henry Stevens, Seymore Wetmore, Delos Waterman, Chas. Walker, John Henning, Wm. H. Brannon, Samuel Bechtelheimer, George Bowker, Dexter Horton, Wm. A. Strickler and Timothy D. Hinckley. H. H. Tobin, Henry Pierce, O. M. Eaton, Henry Van Asselt, Franklin Matthias and Henry L. Yesler appeared as witnesses for the prosecution, while those for the defense were Edward A. Clark, Lewis V. Wyckoff, C. D. Boren, Sidney B. Simons, Luther M. Collins, Wm. H. Brown, Henry Adams, Joseph Williamson and Wm. N. Bell. The whole proceedings were generally looked upon as a joke, but a couple of the jurors and the prosecuting attorney made it as serious for the prisoners as they could. Maurer was tried first, and very much to his relief, and quite as much to his surprise, was acquitted. Several of the Grand Jurors, it will be noticed, were witnesses for the defense, while Maurer himself was one of the regular panel of Petit Jurors, he being excused, of course, from trying himself, as Heebner had been from indicting himself. Heebner's trial followed Maurer's, occurring on the 1st of November. The jurors then were Seymore Wetmore, T. D. Hinckley, Delos Waterman, Henry Stevens, Henry H. Decker, Daniel J. Sackman, John Hograve, Tarkington Sower, Arthur A. Denny, John Jameson, Wm. A. Strickler and Adolphus Clymer. Heebner was a pretty tough fellow, and a harder fight was made against him than against poor Maurer. Some of the jurors held out for conviction for a long time. Judge Lander was as easy on the prisoners as he could be, without absolutely turning them loose. Joseph Cushman, of Olympia, and W. C. Pease, captain of the U. S. revenue cutter Jeff Davis, were attorneys for the defence. Heebner was acquitted also, whereupon the charge against Collins was dismissed. The witness fees in the Maurer case amounted to $57.70, while there was a charge for meals to jurors of $24; the meals in the Heebner case coming to $42, at 50 cents each, evidently seven table sittings. The court was held in the Felker House, kept then by Mary Ann Boyer, known to all old residents as "Mother Damnable," on account of her fierce temper, profane language and hard character. She was a good cook, had the best house in town, and got the patronage of the traveling public. Lawyer Clark made a stiff fight for conviction of the accused men. He wanted to make a good impression as a lawyer, he being young, and they all new to each other. His course aroused some feeling of unpleasantness, one manifestation thereof, perhaps, being a large bill for accommodations at the Boyer House. He objected to it, but she was firm. He at last paid, but said that he must have a receipt to show, and to prevent her from exacting payment again. As she could neither read nor write she could give no receipt. By this time she was angry, in a rage, and, telling him she would give him a receipt, she stepped back into the kitchen. Returning with several sticks of stovewood she advanced upon Clark with the words: "You want a receipt, do you? Well, you shall have one. Here it is. Take it," letting drive at him with all her great force one of the chunks of wood. He had become aware of her hostile intent, and fled, she pelting him with the sticks as long as he was within sight and range. Clark never afterwards wanted a receipt from her, and when the story got out no one else who heard it cared to risk the experience he then had by similarly annoying her. It is doubtful if the U. S. Marshal, who paid her $39 for furniture and room rent of the court during the short term, had the courage to ask a receipt from her. If he did, it is possible that, being a smooth politician, he adroitly avoided giving her offense. Dr. Maynard had trouble with her about the same time. It was a case of trespass. Justice Holder- ness decided in favor of Mrs. Boyer, but on appeal to the District Court Holderness was reversed and Maynard won.

At the April term, 1855, David S. Maynard was appointed by Judge Chenoweth a U. S. Commissioner, to take acknowledgments, bail affidavits and attend to the other duties of the office. At the October term, in 1856, Elwood Evans, H. R. Crosby and William H. Wallace were appointed by the District Judge, Chenoweth, a committee to examine Maynard with a view to ascertaining his qualifications for practising at the bar as an attorney-at-law. The committee reported to the Court that Maynard was of good moral character, and was qualified in all respects required by the statutes, and recommended that his application for the right to practise law be granted. The Judge accepted the report, and on the 28th Maynard was sworn in to support the Constitution of the United States and the laws of the Territory of Washington, and to demean himself faithfully and honestly as an attorney, counselor and solicitor. After this term (October, 1856), the court in Seattle was abolished, and not revived or renewed until February, 1864.

Though Mesatchee Jim was much disliked by other Indians, and they were glad to be rid of him, they believed that the white men should be punished for his hanging, and they were disappointed when Maurer, Heebner and Collins were released. As some sort of compensation for the killing of Jim, they went over to the ranch of a lonely old bachelor, commonly known as "Old Jack' on the west side of the Duwamish river near its mouth, and killed him. In a general way the justice of the act of retribution upon the whites was recognized among the people, looking at it from the Indian standpoint, and no attempt was ever made to punish "Old Jack's" murderers. Deterrent effect upon the vengeance of the settlers was also caused by the fact that two other Indians had recently been given the same treatment that Mesatchee Jim had received, for crimes they were supposed to have committed. Further, it began to look like a dangerous game longer to play. The honor of the County School Superintendency was bestowed upon

Dr. Maynard about this time, being added to his numerous other official and public favors.

Maynard
Doctor
Blacksmith
Plat owner
Attorney
County School Superintendent

THE TREATY OF POINT ELLIOTT

ON the 20th of January, 1855, and for three days following, a council was held at Point Elliott, near the present city of Everett, by Gov. Stevens with the head men of the Duwamish, Suquamish, Snohomish, Snoqualmie, Skagit and other tribes further north, including Seattle, Patkanim, Goliah and Chowittshoot. Stevens was accompanied by M. T. Simmons, B. F. Shaw, C. H. Mason, George Gibbs, S. S. Ford, H. D. Cock, Lafayette Balch, E. S. Fowler, H. A. Goldsborough, J. H. Scranton, L. M. Collins, D. S. Maynard and others, the only steamer on Puget Sound, the Major Tompkins, being used for the purpose of the expedition. After considerable talking, feasting, handshaking, smoking and negotiating, a treaty was effected by which the natives relinquished their rights in the greater part of the lands bordering the Sound, accepting as their own places of future residence reservations at a number of different points. For this and promises of peace and good behavior the Indians were to receive instruction in farming, carpentry and the like, free schools were to be established, $15,000 were to be spent in improvements on the reservations, and for twenty years blankets, cloths, and other goods to the amount of $7,500 per annum were to be given. To Maynard one of the gratifying features of the council was the good feeling evinced towards him by many of the natives. In making the first talk for the Indians at the conference, Seattle

69

concluded with these words: "My mind is like yours. I don't want to say more. My heart is very good towards Dr. Maynard. I want always to get medicine from him." Chowittshoot, of Bellingham Bay, wound up with: "My mind is the same as Seattle's. I love him and send my friends to him if they are sick. I go to Dr. Maynard at Seattle if I am sick." The Governor promised them a doctor, as the desire for one was expressed by each and all of the chiefs. Maynard was the appointee, later in the year. The treaty was not ratified by the U. S. Senate until 1859, and, of course, the promised benefactions did not reach the Indians. They did not understand this, and complained and protested at the delay. In January, 1856, when the first year's goods were due, the Indian war was at its height. The Indian superintendent and his agents did not know what to do. In his desire to keep at least partial faith with the red men, or at any rate have them think that he was doing so, Agent Maynard bought $1,300 worth of goods from Plummer & Chase, Seattle merchants, and distributed them among the natives as the they were a part of the promised government bounty or payment for the lands. As this was not in accordance with custom and regulation, the Department at Washington never could find a way for settling this claim of Maynard's, and he lost the whole amount.

THE WAR OF 1855-56

THE Indians of Eastern Washington became seriously disaffected in the summer of 1855. Their mutterings at first were disregarded. The army officers and some of the officials of the Territory would not believe there was danger. As time went on the feelings of discontent and hostility were insidiously and diligently spread among the natives in the western half of the Territory and throughout the Territory of Oregon. Finally there were overt acts of war. A party of gold seekers from Seattle, bound for a reported mining district in the vicinity of Colville, were attacked in the Yakima country. Several of the^ men were killed, and the others escaped to tell the tale. An Indian agent was sent to investigate the matter and demand the punishment of the murderers. He, too, was killed. A hundred soldiers next went into the country of the hostiles, only to be attacked and driven back with considerable loss. The war was now on, and its scene was rapidly extended to the west, particularly to the country included within the limits of King County. Attacks were made upon the whites at a number of places, citizens of the Territory, U. S. soldiers and settlers—men, women and children—being slain, houses burned, and other property ruined and destroyed. The town of Seattle was fortified, and though the citizens were assisted in its defense by a ship of war with one hundred and fifty men on board and on shore, it was attacked by the savages, and a desperate battle fought for its capture on the one side and its protection on the other. Gov. Stevens, who was also Superintendent of Indian Affairs, evolved the idea of separating the Indians, the hostiles from the friendlies or the supposed friendlies. In furtherance of that plan he established several camps on the islands and on the west shore of the Sound, into which he gathered as many Indians as possible, placing them under the care of agents, feeding them, and keeping from them as far as possible the emissaries of the enemy. For this purpose he looked up men for agents who were discreet, who possessed the confidence of the Indians, and who could be relied upon to do what was right by them and by the government and people. One of the men so selected was Doctor Maynard. He was given charge of the Indians of Seattle, Shilshole bay, Port Orchard and Port Madison, with headquarters at the latter place, upon the reservation set aside for his old friend, Chief Seattle, and the tribe of Suquamishes. There Maynard watched and cared for the Indians for a year and a half, making frequent trips to the other points of refuge, and carrying out the idea of the Governor most successfully and completely. Several thousand Indians were in his charge, who would have given a vast deal of trouble had they put on the war paint and joined Owhi, Leschi, Kanasket, Kitsap and their associates. In this way the services of the men of peace were no less valuable than were those of the men of war; in fact, they may have been infinitely more valuable to the weak settlements then scattered along the shores of Puget

Sound, saving some of them from destruction that otherwise could not have been averted. While so engaged Maynard was also attending to professional calls from his neighbors, and was by no means neglecting his duties as an officer of the Court and as a citizen. They were trying times to all, and no less so to him than to others, though he gave little evidence of worry, owing to his hearty, jovial, good nature.

EVENTS OF 1859-'60

THE war being ended, Maynard returned to town. Conditions had greatly changed. The farms of the country had been practically destroyed, but little more than the land being left. Homes in town had been similarly treated. Quite a number of the survivors either had already left the country or were then preparing to leave. The population was much reduced. There was almost no business. Money was exceedingly scarce. It was difficult, indeed, to live in the ordinary way. The town was set back for several years. There was no demand for lots. In fact, there were many more lots than there were people, and some of the discouraged ones were led to believe and say that land enough was already platted and sold for all the town that ever would be seen at Seattle. Maynard, being of hopeful disposition, and inclined to optimism, was unable to share in the gloomy views of his fellow townsfolk. At the same time he could not endure a life of sloth and inaction. His thoughts turned to the soil, and he began to talk of the pleasant life of the farmer. He was sure that if he were a tiller of the soil he would be prosperous as well as happy. Visions of the orchard, the vegetable garden, the poultry, the horses and cattle were before him. The more he thought of these things the more he wanted his visions realized. He did not reflect that he had land enough, and good land, for this purpose. He must have another place, out of town, in the country, and yet nearby, where he could

74

maintain his agricultural operations and still, if he chose, make a few dollars occasionally from the practise of his profession among his old neighbors. While in this frame of mind he fell in with Charley Terry. Terry was the keenest and shrewdest of the local pioneers, full of energy and action, and one who knew a good thing the moment he saw it. In trading Maynard was no match for him. It did not take Terry long to effect an exchange of his Alki Point claim of 319 acres for the 260 acres of Maynard's claim then unplatted. On the nth of July, 1857, they passed deeds each to the other, Terry acquiring land by the transaction worth today an average, perhaps, of $100,000 an acre, while Maynard got land that possibly might sell for $3,000 an acre. In other words the land that Terry got is now worth not far from $26,000,000, while the land that Maynard got is worth $1,000,000. The Doctor and his wife moved over to Alki and lived there for several years. They had a good home, and they endeavored to make the place attractive to visitors, having company frequently, and doing considerable in the way of hospitality. His place was a port of call for boatmen on the way up and down the Sound, while the Indians, always glad to see their old friend, camped there almost continually, and fed upon him until he had little left for himself and wife, and nothing to sell. Though he talked loud and often about the free and happy life of the farmer; sent samples of his finest garden stuff to the Olympia and Steilacoom newspapers, in illustration of what could be grown on the Sound, and kept up appearances generally, he became discouraged after five or six years' trials, and was rather glad to get back to town, especially after the burning of his farmhouse and contents. Upon resumption of life in Seattle, the Doctor tried to sell the Alki farm. Men would look at it, but would not pay the price. Year by year the latter was reduced, until in 1868 (Sept. 28th), he found a man who was willing, able and sufficiently courageous to pay him $450 for the 314 acres of land then remaining. This venturesome individual was Knud Olson, known to all the old settlers from his long residence on the Alki place. A few days later Olson bought 161 acres adjoining, now in West Seattle, from George Bannock, for $300. These prices give an idea of how little value, less than forty years ago, was connected with Seattle property now worth millions almost beyond computation.

While Maynard was on the farm it is not to be supposed that he was doing nothing in the town or for the country. In illustration of his life during the six years there, 1859 may be referred to. That year he was appointed Court Commissioner for King County, and was also elected Justice of the Peace for Seattle precinct. There still being no resident minister of the gospel in the village, Justice Maynard's services were frequently availed of by the young men and women who were spoiling for matrimony. On the 28th of August he made two couples happy, no previous day in local annals equaling that in this respect. Lewis V. Wyckoff and Mrs. Ursula McConaha were then legally

76

joined by him, in the home of the widow, while at the Terry residence Capt. John S. Hill and Miss Addie J. Andrews were also married. A fortnight later (Sept. 15th, 1859,) Miss Nellie M. Andrews, a sister of Mrs. Hill, and Sumner B. Hinds were married by Justice Maynard.

These young ladies were from Bucksport, Maine, and had been on the Sound but a short time. Hinds's partner, Charles Plummer, was also married by Maynard, at Alki, on the 4th of July, 1860, the bride being Mrs. Sarah J. Harris, not long from Lowell, Massachusetts. Plummer, by the way, was one of the most enterprising men in Seattle, who believed in doing in the best manner whatever he attempted. The dwelling that he built was the finest of its day, his store building and hall were the same, and so likewise were his hotel building, wharf and other undertakings.

On the 22d of July, 1859, John H. Scranton gave to the Olympia and Steilacoom people the opportunity of coming to Seattle on the new steamer Julia for the low price (at the time) of three dollars a person. Two hundred people availed themselves of the privilege. Scranton advertised up the Sound one of the attractions as follows:

"In order to give zest to the entertainment, Dr. Maynard, hyas tyee of the Seattle tribe of Indians, will superintend the grand clam bake. The clams and other shellfish will be

77

cooked on heated stones in the ancient style of the aborigines of our Territory."

Seattle people made every effort to properly receive and care for their guests. A salute was fired from the wharf. Mrs. Terry threw open her house to the upper Sound ladies. The attractions of the town then consisted of the three wharfs—Yesler's, Horton's and Plummer's; the Woodin tannery; the Methodist church; the Yesler saw mill and cook house, and the old blockhouse fort, in addition to the stores, hotels and—saloons. Capt. A. C. Rand seemed to head the committee on reception and entertainment, members of which were the townsmen and townswomen generally. A free ball and supper were given in the Plummer Hall at night. All went on successfully and happily except the grand event—the clam bake. To the great disappointment of the citizens, and to Maynard's utter humiliation, the tides served badly. For several days they refused to go out so as to uncover the beds, and it was found to be impossible to obtain the shellfish requisite for this feature of the day's program, upon which such great expectations had been based.

It will be pardonable on the part of the author to say that the occasion of this excursion was his first visit to Seattle. His two older brothers and father were of the company. We boys, after looking over the town—the task of a few minutes only—decided that in standard Seattle was not up to our own Steilacoom. It was not so large, so well built, so clean, so handsome. Many of the houses were unpainted; not one was plastered. By comparison we were proud of our home place. Seattle was not and never would be the equal of Steilacoom. Our exultation was beyond suppression or concealment. The town boys with whom we came in contact intuitively and otherwise were made aware of our feelings. They resented them. More than forty years afterwards C. H. Hanford, the present U. S. District Judge, told me that he and his young neighbors were then very anxious to tone us down; they believing that we were too cocky, and that a ride on a rail, ducking in the slough, Sunday clothes and all, and other performances of like character, were due us as a part of our just entertainment, the lack of opportunity only preventing our receiving the full measure of our desserts at their hands. Steilacoom is today just as populous as it was then, and of less general importance. Seattle is—well, everybody knows.

For many years Puget Sounders believed there was much gold on the eastern slope of the Cascade mountains, in what are now Kittitas, Chelan, Okanogan, Ferry and Stevens counties and Southern British Columbia, and every year there was talk of Swauk, Colville, Similkameen, Rock Creek, Wenatchee and other places where it was supposed to be. Prospectors went there, and occasionally brought back exciting and sensational reports—50 cents and $1 to the pan, and $20 to $100 a day to the man. Seattle was eager to get a road thru the mountains, that it might share in the trade benefits sure some time to be derived. On the 20th of August a meeting was held for the purpose of getting the Snoqualmie road opened. Capt. Rand was chairman, Jasper W. Johnson, secretary, and L. D. Harris was made treasurer. J. C. Kellogg, A. A. Denny, F. Matthias, H. L. Yesler, D. S. Maynard and others were present. It was determined to open the road from the Snoqualmie Prairie to the eastern side, and the job was placed in the hands of Timothy D. Hinckley. Maynard, Yesler and Matthias, as a committee, were put in general charge, and they expended $1,350 in opening the road to a point seven miles east of Lake Kichelas. They issued a report in which they told what had been done, and praised the route as central, practicable and available for immigrants, miners, traders and travelers to and from Seattle or the country to the south and north. The next year there was quite a rush to the Rock Creek diggings, and to other streams on the way. Plummer & Hinds sent two pack trains of fifteen animals each. Robert Russell, Thomas S. Russell, Joseph Foster, J. C. Kellogg, Low, Richard, King and others went. The Yesler mill was short handed in consequence of the exodus. A single party numbered twenty-five men. It looked good for a few weeks. Portland, Victoria and Seattle planned and fixed themselves for a great rush of miners. But, like too many such affairs, it did not "pan out," and by the end of the season was known to be one more of the long list of mining failures.

RETURN TO SEATTLE

UPON resuming his residence in town, Maynard began about where he had left off. One of the first things I was to start the King County Agricultural Society, in June, 1863. Then with Christian Clymer, Thomas M. Alvord, Josiah H. Settle, Joseph Williamson, D. A. Neeley, Francis McNatt, Edmund Carr, S. F. Coombs and others the Society was organized. Maynard for a time was secretary and Clymer president. To reopen the hospital was another idea. From the earliest days he had occupied the field as physician and surgeon to the fullest extent possible. He had cared for the sane and the insane, the sick and the maimed, when no one else could or would. This was far back in the 50's. Now in the 60's he resumed the difficult and disagreeable burden. In the first issue of the first Seattle newspaper—the Gazette of December 10th, 1863—appeared his advertisement as physician and surgeon, and the additional announcement that the Seattle Hospital would be opened on the 15th. The further statement was made that in connection with the hospital the lying-in apartment would be under the care of Mrs. C. T. Maynard, aided by suitable nurses. A fortnight later, the editor, J. R. Watson, mentioned a supper given at the Union Hotel to himself and friends by Dr. Maynard, who was said to have been that evening in one of his happiest, story-telling moods. The "boys" thought it a good joke on the Doctor to inveigle him into a funny society under the delusion that he was joining a secret organization devoted to the advancement of his political principles. He was surprised at the ludicrous character of the initiation, but he kept his temper and pretended to enjoy it as much as those engaged in directing and watching the mysterious performances. When A. S. Mercer arrived with his first company of young women from the Atlantic they were given a public reception, at which Dr. Maynard presided, Rev. Nehemiah Doane making an address of welcome, and Mercer responding for the ladies. Maynard was a devoted Mason, and promptly joined the first Seattle Lodge—St. John's, organized in 1860. One of the last acts of his life was to deed to St. John's Lodge one of the very few lots he yet had remaining in his "town of Seattle." Shortly before his death the Masons determined upon having a cemetery. Maynard was one of the men who selected the land—the present Lakeview—and his own was the first body that was there interred. Among the later organizations of Seattle in which he took interest were the Seattle Library Association, and the first Society of Pioneers. Though an admitted attorney-at-law he made but little effort in that direction. In 1865, however, he formed a partnership with E. L. Bridges, as Maynard & Bridges, opening an office, and offering to practise as attorneys and counselors-at-law in all the courts of the Territory. In 1870 he and Dr. Rust were associated in partnership as physicians. Of course, in a work like this it is impossible to mention more than a few of the deeds and associations of the subject of the narrative. For this reason many matters—some of importance and interest—concerning Dr. Maynard are necessarily omitted, and others reduced to the shortest possible mention.

STRIVES TO GET LAND TITLE

DURING all these years Maynard had been unable to perfect title to his land. He began promptly, and did all that he could, but there were delays at Washington City to this day beyond understanding. He laid claim to 640 acres, in as nearly a square shape as possible, under the provisions of the first Oregon Donation Act, that of September 27, 1850. By the terms of this act, and of later acts amendatory of it, a man who was a resident of Oregon on or before December 1, 1850, was entitled to 320 acres of land on his own account, and if he were married then or within one year of that date his wife would also be entitled to 320 acres, they being settlers and occupants of the public lands. A positive requirement of the law was that notice should be given by the settler of his claim on or before the 1st of December, 1855, those who did not give such notice being forever debarred from the benefit of the law. Maynard wanted the 320 acres for his wife, and he tried to get the land for her, the he apparently realized the difficulty in the way of so doing. The first Mrs. Maynard complied with none of the terms; not residing upon the land herself, and being divorced before title inured to him. The second Mrs. Maynard might have obtained the land as the widow of Israel Broshears, but she made no such effort; she might also have obtained it as the wife of Maynard, had she married him sooner. Tho efforts were made in behalf of both women, both lost. Doctor Maynard accompanied his application with the necessary affidavit, made before H. L. Yesler, as Clerk of the Probate Court of King County, on the 26th of October, 1853, in which he told of both wives and both marriages, and gave the other necessary information. He used the expression that he "was intermarried with Lydia A. Maynard, his first wife, until December 24th, 1852," and further on said that he "is intermarried with Catherine T. Broshears, his second wife, and that he was legally married to her on the 15th day of January, 1853." There was no intended deception in these statements,' but years afterwards the government land officers misunderstood the first one, and reported that Maynard had sworn that his first wife had died on the 24th of December, 1852. Bancroft and others have used this statement to the detriment of Maynard's reputation. Without entering into the detail of his divorce, he meant neither more nor less than he said, saying it in as few words as possible. The erroneous impression of the land officers put upon him the odium of a perjuror, which it is well here to remove. After he had been upon the land four years, as required, he made proof of residence from April 3d, 1852, to April 3d, 1856, and thirteen years later, May 14th, 1869, the Register and Receiver at Olympia issued certificate to David S. and Catherine T. Maynard, the husband to have the west half of the claim and the wife the east half. Two years later the Commissioner of the General Land Office got around to this case. When he saw the statement about Lydia A. Maynard he concluded at once

Lydia trouble!

that she had been upon the land, that she had died there, and that the half section belonged to her estate. He accordingly (July 21st, 1871,) returned the papers to the Olympia office, and directed the officials there to make inquiries along the lines he indicated, particularly as to the heirs of the deceased Lydia A. Maynard. The Register and Receiver held this investigation on the 6th of March, 1872, when Lydia A. Maynard herself appeared before them, proved her marriage, and made demand for the apportionment to her of one-half the Maynard claim of 640 acres, asking that it be cut into north and south halves and one of the two assigned to her. She was represented by Col. C. H. Larrabee, as attorney, or by Larrabee & White, partners. Mr. James McNaught represented the opposition, in behalf of the Terry estate, Hugh McAleer and others who had bought from Maynard and did not want to lose their properties. The upshot of it at Olympia was that Register Clark and Receiver Stuart found that Lydia A. Maynard was entitled to one-half the claim, and they awarded her the east half, taking into account the fact that Maynard had sold all of the west half but two town lots, and that making division of the land into north and south halves would entail upon innocent parties a great deal of needless trouble. Before these proceedings at Olympia, however, there had been much agitation at Seattle for several months. A deed was filed from Lydia A. Maynard to Larrabee and two strangers on the 18th of November, 1871, of her right, title, interest and demand to

86

her one-half part of David S. Maynard's donation claim. This was done by her as "the wife of David S. Maynard." The lawyer thought, perhaps, that this latter statement weakened the deed, as shortly after another deed was received from her substantially the same as the first in which that statement was omitted. In March, 1872, Lydia A. Maynard gave to Larrabee a strong and sweeping power of attorney to represent her and her interests in securing the wife's one-half part of the claim, to demand patent, plat, sell, and so forth. Of course, all this made much commotion in Seattle. The people chiefly concerned did not know what to say or do to protect their rights and save their landed possessions. The whole proceeding was regarded with disfavor, and those engaged in it were viewed with suspicion. It was explained and reexplained and promises were made of conciliatory character. It was felt that if the new claimant from Wisconsin won her case the people of Seattle would have to pay. Quite a number went to her and got deeds, under the apprehension that she had rights in the land, and that the prudent thing to do was to deal with her in the beginning. Attorney McNaught, at Washington City, presented to the Commissioner of the General Land Office the appeal from that portion of the decision awarding to Lydia A. Maynard a half interst in the claim and the apportionment to her of the east half thereof. The Commission, on the 12th of August, decided in favor of D. S. Maynard for the west half of the claim, but against both women. Appeal being taken to the Secretary of the

Interior, he, Columbus Delano, affirmed the decision of the Commissioner on the 1st of March, 1873. He found that "Maynard had fully complied with all the requirements of the law relating to settlement and cultivation." The title had not vested in him at the time of the divorce, the legality of which was not questioned, and Lydia A. Maynard could claim no interest in the land by virtue of her wifehood. Nor had she ever been upon the land, and therefore had no claim in her own right. The conditions prescribed by the law "not having been complied with at the time of the divorce, the interest of Lydia in the premises was terminated by the dissolution of the marriage contract with David." As for the second wife the decision was that she was "not entitled because she was not the wife of the applicant on the first day of December, 1850, or within one year from that date. The act was evidently intended to limit the additional 320 acres to cases where the person was married before the 1st of December, 1851." This decision ended the contention as far as the west half of the claim was concerned. The fight for the east half spread over a period of thirty years, and was engaged in by the city of Seattle, Hugh McAleer, C. M. Bywater, the heirs of Lydia A. Maynard, Harry C. Algar, J. Vance Lewis and W. C. Hill. With the help of attorneys and under the various land laws the struggle was carried before the land officials of the government and in the courts, the claimants one after another being eliminated until their number was reduced to the three last named, to whom awards were ultimately made. It may be truthfully said that including taxes, the cost of litigation and all other expenses, this land has to this date been of more burden than benefit to its claimants and possessors—something that cannot be said of land elsewhere in the city of Seattle. The issuance of patent to the Doctor's half of the claim was delayed three years longer, until the 14th of December, 1876. He had then been long in his grave, and was therefore denied the satisfaction of witnessing the final outcome of his efforts to secure a Donation claim, of holding in his hand the deed from the government promised him by the law nearly a quarter of a century before. May-- nard was the only one of the original Seattle town site claimants who was entitled to the larger bounty of the government—640 acres—and he was also the only one who was deprived of the half of the land promised him by reason of his migration to and settlement in the country in 1850. The outcome was pitiful, but it seemed to be unavoidable.

DEATH CLAIMS

WHETHER or not his troubles during the years 1871-
'72-'73 hastened his death cannot, of course, be told. It is
not at all unlikely that they did. He bore up under them
bravely, presented to the public as strong a front as
possible, and was as light hearted, or pretended to be, as
ever. The burden he carried was a heavy one, and in the
end it proved too much for his strength. A physical ailment
was aggravated. He weakened rapidly, and on Thursday
evening, March 13th, 1873, his spirit took its flight. The
tender, compassionate feelings of the community were
aroused in his behalf, and at his demise there was' general
and generous exhibition of them. The funeral services were
held in the Yesler pavilion on the 15th, conducted by Rev.
John F. Damon, and participated in by all the town. Places
of business were closed. The procession was headed by the
Seattle band, and two of the principal features of it were St.
John's and Kane Lodges of Masons. The new Masonic
cemetery not being ready, the body of the Doctor for a few
days was placed in the toolhouse of the old cemetery, now
known as Denny Park. His first wife, Lydia A., did not long
survive him, she dying at her home in Wisconsin in 1875.
The second wife, Catherine T., is yet (1906) living.

90

CHARACTERISTICS AND ANECDOTES OF MAYNARD

DOCTOR DAVID S. MAYNARD was a man of marked individuality and of strong characteristics. He was richly endowed with good qualities. No one could be more liberal and kind than he. This disposition on his part constantly led to impoverishment. He could not say no to those asking his services, his moneys, his lands and personal possessions. Had others treated him as well as he treated them he would have been rich all his life, and instead of dying poor would have left one of the best estates in the Territory. He was fearless. There was evidence of this from the beginning. It showed very plainly in the long, dangerous trip across the continent. The lack of money, the cholera, Indians, storms, rough waters were to all appearances the same to him as the ordinary and less exciting or depressing events of the road. In war, in peace, in business, in all the affairs of life, he was the same hearty, courageous man. He was affectionate. Though he separated from his first wife the fault is not believed to have been his. He treated her better than she treated him. Not a word did he at any time utter against her, nor did he ever do anything hostile to her interests. He cared for his children tenderly until they were grown, and afterwards did what he could for them, the his abilities then were small. The second Mrs. Maynard was always sure there was no better man on earth. His good nature and good humor were unfailing and irrepressible. The day his first wife came to

91

Seattle, in March, 1872, he stepped into the barber shop, and said: "Dixon, fix me up in your best style." "What's up, Doctor? What are you going to do?" "I am going to give the people here a sight they never had before, and may never have again. I'm going to show them a man walking up the street with a wife on each arm." Sure enough; when the steamer came in from the upper Sound Maynard and his second wife were there to meet the first wife, and they walked together to his home where they dwelt until Lydia A. left on her return to Wisconsin, somewhat to the surprise and amusement of the general public. One would not suppose that he would have felt at all jocose under the circumstances, but if he did not there was no betrayal of his real feelings. He was a home buyer, a protectionist, a friend to his nearest neighbors. Stepping into a shop one day he told the keeper, whom he had been patronizing for years, that he would not see him there anymore. "Why, Doctor? What's the matter?" inquired his astonished friend. "We are going to have a shop in Maynardtown, and I always stand by my own side and help my own people," the Doctor replied. The shop he was giving up was on Yesler's land, about sixty feet from "Maynardtown." It was always this way with him. He favored the United States above all other nations; Washington Territory above all other American commonwealths; Seattle above all other towns or cities; and his own nearest neighbors above all other peoples. In his willingness, or desire, to help the needy, the unhappy, the unfortunate, he sometimes went too far, beyond the

92

limits of prudence and wisdom. A youthful pair from the upper Sound one day made sudden appeal to him. They were anxious to marry; the girl's father had refused his consent, and they were sure he was then pursuing them, his objection being her lack of age. Maynard's sympathies were at once excited. He wrote on two pieces of paper the figures "18," and saw the girl put them on the inside soles of her shoes. When the minister, being doubtful, asked as to her age, Maynard said that he did not know exactly, but he was sure "she was over 18." Not long after the angry father came along, and he both censured and threatened the Rev. Daniel Bagley for what he had done. The preacher took him to Dr. Maynard, who laughingly told of the stratagem he had practised and proceeded to justify it. As is the case generally in such affairs, the parent was compelled to accept the situation, and, dropping his opposition, make the best of it. Maynard's course in this affair was one that the most friendly biographer could not excuse. It illustrates, however, one of the most prominent features of his character, that led him more often to the commission of good acts than of bad. As a physician Seattle had no better during his time. He was one of the olden school, not the modern, which relies too much upon surgery, upon the use of the knife and the saw. Nor was he a great medicine doser. He depended largely upon the most simple means—upon pleasant surroundings, a cheerful atmosphere, confidence upon the part of the patient, the alleviation of pain, fresh air, sanitary conditions, and

93

occasionally a bit of pardonable deception. Many a person who imagined himself or herself dangerously ill was cured by him with a prescription of water, disguised, perhaps, by the addition of a little salt or other harmless ingredient. He wanted people to live well, and he lived well himself, the only exception being the habit of drinking spirituous liquor in excessive quantities; a habit which grew upon him in the later years of his life, but which was never known to result in injury to others. In fact, it was a local joke that Maynard was a better physician when full than when sober, and a similar comparison was often made by the same jokers between him and more temperate physicians, which was very hard for the latter to bear. None of the first people had more enterprise than he. He was the first of many things. In Seattle he was the first of the immigrants, coming one, two or three years before his contemporaries, the first professional man, first official, first employer, first real estate seller, first merchant, the first in and of a great number of movements and undertakings of business, social and public character. There was no holding back with him. If a thing was desirable, he was in favor of it; if wanted, he would go at once; if it had to be done, or it was well to do it, he was ready to devote to it his money to the last dollar. His usefulness in his latter days was considerably lessened by his lack of means. By that time, however, the solidity of the town was established, its great future was assured, and there were others able and willing to direct events and carry the burden without that assistance which he would have gladly given had he been able. Under all the circumstances it is not astonishing that Maynard possessed the sympathies of the people; that they sincerely regretted his misfortunes; that they mourned his departure as that of a true friend and of a public benefactor; and that his memory has remained with his surviving acquaintances green, fresh and pleasant to this day.

CATHERINE TROUTMAN MAYNARD

Born and Reared in Kentucky; Married in Illinois.

A CENTURY ago they had large families in Kentucky. One of these was the Troutman family. Michael Troutman was twice married, and had ten children by each wife. It is said of him that he got together most of his descendants at the home farm, in Bullitt County, on Christmas day of 1813. Ten of his children were present, ninety grandchildren, nineteen great grandchildren, and three great great grandchildren. All of the 122 sat down to dinner with their progenitor in the one dining room, the length of which was eighty feet, the house being a three-story brick as large as a European castle. There probably never was a more remarkable family reunion in the United States. Grandfather Troutman, as he was generally known in his later years, lived to the age of 89, while Grandmother Troutman lived to be 96. Their landed possessions were vast, including, it is stated, 30,000 acres. Another large family was the Simmons's. They lived in Meade County, about twenty miles from Louisville. In its various branches were eight, ten and twelve children. Michael Troutman Simmons was the father of twelve, and his father was one of ten children. They also were well off, having three plantations, one being devoted to cotton, one to hemp and one to corn. Three hundred negro slaves were a part of the

96

Simmons family possessions. The Simmons and Troutman families were allied by marriage.

One of the members of these large and wealthy families was Catherine Troutman Simmons, sister of the Michael T. Simmons referred to. She was born on her mother's plantation in Meade County on the 19th of July, 1816. There she was brought up, educated and lived for fifteen years. Desire for a change came upon them, and in consequence the family moved to Pike County, Illinois, in 1831. Mr. Simmons died, and the mother remarried, her second husband being James

married it 18 yrs

Morton, said to have been a cousin of Senator Morton of Indiana. On the 6th of December, 1832, Catherine was married to Israel Broshears. Her father and mother gave her a grand wedding. There were four bridesmaids and four groomsmen, and a great number of guests, dinner being served to all the company. Broshears was a pilot on the Mississippi river, down to New Orleans. After marriage he became a farmer.

MR and Mrs. Broshears lived in Illinois until 1849. They were then taken with the Pacific coast fever. They prepared that year for the journey across the plains and mountains to Oregon. Michael T. Simmons had gone on ahead, in 1844, and Andrew Jackson Simmons, his brother, had followed five years later. Mr and Mrs. Morton and several other Mortons and Broshears now made ready to go, and with them were Mr. and Mrs. Samuel Rider, she being a Simmons by birth. He was blind. They left Pike County, Illinois, in December, for Jackson County, Missouri, where further arrangements were made for the journey before them. Intending to go slowly, and take plenty of time, they made an early start, on the 22d of March, 1850. It would have been better for them if they had gone more rapidly, as they would then have avoided the cholera which assailed them, with great virulence before they were half way over the road. When near Fort Kearney, the latter part of the first week in June, Israel Broshears was taken with cholera, and after him six members of their party, with fatal results. They inquired for a doctor at once, and were told of one who was riding along on a mule not far away. He was called, being taken first to Mrs. Morton, who was then near death. "Never mind me," she said, "but look after my widowed daughter, my daughter with the blind husband and the others. You can do nothing for me. I am going. Help them, Doctor. Don't desert my children." A stream of rapidly-moving immigrants passed by. "Hurry on!" they shouted. "Leave the dead!" "Save yourselves!". "You'll die if you stop to bury them!"

"Help you? No!" Past the plague spot they went, in abject terror, whipping their animals to hasten their movements to the utmost. But Mrs. Broshears would not go until her husband, her mother and the others were buried by the roadside, their bodies as safe as they could be made from the teeth of wolves and the scalping knives of Indians. The Doctor rendered all the service he could, to the living and to the dead, and then rode on to rejoin his own party. He told of the promise of help that Mrs. Morton had exacted from him, and of his determination to keep his word good by giving to the stricken people all the aid in his power to the end of their journey. Getting together his few things, he returned to the Morton-Broshears-Rider company, placed them in her wagon and took charge. She had five yoke of oxen, two yoke of cows, a large, strong wagon, and a first-class equipment. Had they possessed less there was then opportunity for getting more merely for the taking. The cholera destroyed whole families in some cases, and in others there was such decimation of the trains that it became necessary to leave by the wayside much that could no longer be cared for. Wagons were abandoned in some instances, with all their contents. Goods were thrown out to lighten other vehicles, that faster traveling could be done. In the effort to get away as quickly as possible from the accursed place, every manner of relief was sought. The widow found in the beginning that the Doctor (David S. Maynard) was not a first class teamster. In fact, it was his first experience with an ox team, and to put a novice in charge of seven yoke of cattle under such circumstances was imposing a burden and strain upon him of momentous character. He soon learned the business, however, becoming an expert in the line long before he reached the

99

Columbia river. He made up for lost time; he passed numerous parties on the road, and he drove into The Dalles on the 16th of September. He also was given practise in milking cows, which animals in their way did much to render the trip endurable, and at times pleasant. The Doctor sold the cattle and wagon at The Dalles, and provided for transportation the rest of the way by water to Vancouver and Cowlitz river. Mrs. Broshears found it convenient to leave everything to him. He proved to be thoroly capable, and in every way worthy of the trust. It should be said, however, that on the road they picked up a man by somewhat singular accident who served them faithfully to the end. George Benton, a nephew of Senator Thomas H. Benton, had started with another party which met disaster in the river South Platte. Several wagons and animals were lost at a supposed ford, where the water was both deep and strong. Benton saved his life and his horse, but lost all else, including shoes, coat and hat, and being left entirely alone on one side of the river. He, perhaps, saved the Broshears-Morton people a similar misfortune by pointing out the danger, and he immediately took service with them at $18 a month and clothes, the latter being an advance payment that was absolutely necessary. When he got to Portland Benton went into the timber trade, received high wages, saved his money, and in a few years was comparatively rich. After leaving the canoe on the upper Cowlitz, they rode to John R. Jackson's on horses. He made them welcome, and gave them assistance to Ford's. At Judge Ford's (Sidney S.) they met A. J. Simmons, then on his way from Puget Sound to meet his mother, sisters and other relatives and friends from the East. The story they told him of the calamity that had befallen them, of the losses they had sustained and of the awful troubles they had endured, were a surprise to him he had not contemplated, and a blow of appalling character. The blanket which Mrs. Broshears sat on from the Cowlitz river had a side saddle placed upon it at Judge Ford's, and the remainder of the ride into Olympia was thereby rendered much more comfortable.

WHEN Mrs. Broshears arrived at Olympia, on the 25th of September, 1850, she found it a very insignificant place, in the first days of its existence as a town, or a settlement called a town. Prior to this date, Newmarket was the center of population and trade for the upper Sound. It was two miles further inland, on the Deschutes river and at its mouth. There, on a claim located by Michael T. Simmons, had been built small saw and grist mills, on account of the water power, and in addition were a store, a few dwellings, and close by, on Bush prairie, several farms. The name was afterwards changed from Newmarket to Tumwater. Simmons had recently sold the greater part of his properties and rights there to Capt. Clanrick Crosby, for $35,000, and about the time of the coming of his relatives had moved down to the new place, then started by Edmund Sylvester. Sylvester was so anxious to get Simmons and his store that he gave the necessary land, two lots, at First and Main streets, where Simmons built a two-story house of 20 by 40 feet, in which he opened a store, having taken in a partner named Chas. Hart Smith. Smith was a smart fellow, who bought the store goods in San Francisco, who sold them at Olympia, and who, if he had remained and been honest, would undoubtedly have been one of the leading men of the Territory and State of Washington. It is said to have been through his insistence that the town was called Olympia, Isaac N. Ebey suggesting the name instead of Smithfield, by which the place had been known for a number of years. Simmons & Smith made money fast, and after a couple of years Smith went to San Francisco to again buy goods, taking cash and credits to the amount of $60,000, belonging chiefly to the two Simmons's and Joseph Broshears. He kept the money and never returned, his associates too late learning that his act was only a breach of trust and not criminally punishable. M. T. Simmons was ruined pecuniarily. During the two or three years Mrs. Broshears lived there, Olympia grew, a hotel being built by Sylvester, other places of business being opened, a newspaper established, and the place becoming known as the chief town of Northern Oregon. Simmons, by far the most prominent man, endeavored to keep his mercantile affairs going. He was postmaster. In partnership with Hugh A. Goldsborough he was trying to do business in real estate, and they were also ship agents. In September, 1852, they were advertising a ship from

London, the John Brewer, and they were also offering cargo space on her for the return trip. Elwood Evans, Parker & Colter, George A. Barnes, W. W. Miller, S. P. Moses, Quincy A. Brooks, Samuel D. Howe, Wm. Billings, Chas. E. Weed, the Sargents, Close, Williams and many others settled there, or near there, during the time referred to. M. M. Smith sailed a boat, called by him a yacht, named the Laplete, carrying Smith's Express, passengers and freight from Olympia to Port Townsend, by way of Poe's Point, Johnson's Ranch, Nisqually, Steilcoom, New York and Whidby Island. Seattle and Tacoma were not on Capt. Smith's map.

NOTWITHSTANDING the newness of things and their primitive character, life at the upper end of Puget Sound was not uninteresting to the widow. Men were many enough compared wth women, there probably being three or four to one. Women were correspondingly in favor. Nothing was too good for them. They could have what they wished for the asking. Mrs. Broshears soon found herself to be in high favor with the bachelors and widowers, and she was evidently regarded by them as a "catch" of the best character. Her people speedily saw the trend of affairs, and they tried to direct it into quarters to suit themselves and their own ideas of propriety and personal desirability. They found out that the beginning of a romance had developed on the plains, east of the Rocky Mountains, and that it had attained with the passage of weeks and months such life

103

and strength as to be quite serious. Knowing that Dr. Maynard was a married man, from his own admissions, they disapproved the bent of inclination shown by him and their widowed sister. They made suggestions of other men, introduced them, arid did what they could to break up the contemplated alliance between Maynard and Mrs. Broshears. They restrained her somewhat of her liberty, and prevented her going with him when they could. More than once they were on the verge of stopping by force the marriage. Mrs. Rider threatened to shoot Dr. Maynard. The latter was not intimidated, no more by white men and women than by Indians or disease. Though M. T. Simmons was a foot the taller- of the two, and a giant in strength, he was unable to alarm or keep away the Doctor. The latter offered to get a divorce. When he left Ohio he said he did not intend to go back to his wife. She understood that they were separated; he knew that they were. He would treat Mrs. Broshears honorably, would marry with her, and in most correct manner would end the trouble. The widow told her relatives that she would marry Dr. Maynard or no one. He went to California; returned to Olympia; moved to Seattle; got his divorce from the Oregon Legislature, and on the 15th of January, 1853, he and Mrs. Broshears were married near Bush Prairie, in Thurston County, by the Rev. Benjamin F. Close, in the presence of A. J. Simmons, Gabriel Jones and wife, and Joseph Broshears and wife. Five days later they were at their new home in the new town of Seattle. It would have been vastly better for their

arrive in Seattle
as newlyweds

sister if the Simmons opposition to her second marriage had not been so prolonged. She was entitled to 320 acres of government land in her own personal right as a "settler or occupant" She was also entitled to the land as the widow of Israel Broshears. And further, she would have been entitled to it as the wife of David S. Maynard. There was a time condition to each of these provisions of the law. She was prevented from exercising the rights first mentioned, and the last one, as Mrs. Maynard, was lost through delay alone. If she had been married on or before the 1st of December, 1851, as she wanted to be, she would have secured 320 acres of land in the city of Seattle worth today two million or more dollars. It was very unfortunate for her. It also involved her in innumerable and distressing troubles needless here to specially mention. Her case illustrates how liable people are to err when their intentions are the very best and they are exercising the utmost possible caution.

AFTER her experience in Illinois, on the plains and in Thurston County, Mrs. Maynard was prepared to pioneer it anywhere. She assumed the duties of her new position at once, uncomplainingly, with the understanding that she was located for life at a point where a great city was to be built, and that she was a partner n the enterprise and was to be one of the helpers in the work. So she sold goods in the store, induced people to locate in their part of the town, as nurse helped her husband in his professional business, and did whatever she could to advance his plans and increase their mutual prosperity. In September, 1853, she went with Dr. Maynard up Duwamish river, and thence by Black river to Lake Washington, she being the first white woman to see or touch the waters of that lake, this being on the 20th of the month. Dr. Maynard, according to her, was the person who gave the name to what is now known as Cedar river and lake. In 1854 she and her husband visited San Francisco, going and returning by sail vessel. One of the first persons Mrs. Maynard here became acquainted with was the daughter of her husband's Indian friend, Seattle, the woman to whom later attached the name Angeline. The two women were about the same age, though Angeline always looked the older. Mrs. Maynard gave her new acquaintance instructions in modern housewifery, and it was under her guidance that Angeline became an expert washerwoman, enabling her to assist the women of the town in their laundry work until her increasing age and debilities compelled her to cease. Their friendship continued warm and intimate to the end of the Indian woman's life, more than forty years later.

THE coming on of the Indian war of 1855~'56 interfered greatly with the growth of the town and the plans of the townspeople, including the Maynards. The Doctor was appointed as agent in charge of the Indians at Seattle and in the vicinity, but with place of residence and office on the reservation near Port Madison. There, surrounded by fifteen hundred Indians and with thousands more within twenty miles, many of whom were openly hostile and more secretly so, he and his wife dwelt for a year and a half, the only people of their race on or near the ground. They had the friendship of Chief Seattle, and he had absolute control and power over the natives under him. So, as far as his tribe was concerned, the Maynards were safe. In addition, they had the protection of that thing of mystery to the savages—the government—and besides the Doctor, as agent, was in constant receipt and had the distribution of rations. The Indians were not like the individual who killed the goose that laid the golden eggs. The man who had the rations to give out was safe among them except in the case of hostile visitors, fanatics or other excited, unbalanced creatures. More, still, the Doctor was a "medicine man," with an influence thereby of unquestioned character, added to which was the recollection of past favors, courage of high order and politic manners impressive and pleasing to the red men. During the progress of hostilities Chief Seattle kept in constant touch with the Indians in and about the town named after him. He was aware of the doings and plans of Leschi, Nelson, Patka-nim and the rest, from his messengers, who in turn went freely among both natives and settlers. TTn the 25th of January, 1856, he knew that a large number of warlike Indians were hovering in the woods back of the town, waiting favorable opportunity to make attack, and, if possible, capture the place and destroy it and its people. He communicated his

107

knowl-Y edge to Agent Maynard. At the same time Gov. Stevens, accompanied by Capt. E. D. Keyes, in command of Fort Steilcoom, M. T. Simmons, Truman H. Fuller and others, was on board the United States Steamer Active, in the harbor of Seattle, counselling with the people of the town and with Capt. Guert Gansevoort, of the United States Ship Decatur, as to the war and the local situation. Stevens believed, or pretended to believe, that there was no immediate danger at Seattle, and he went on to the north to visit the reservations he had in view. At the Port Madison reservation he invited Dr. Maynard to join the party, but the Doctor declined, saying that his presence on the reservation was of some importance, but that on the ship it would be of none, and that he feared trouble was near at hand. The Active steamed on. The agent and his wife discussed the situation, and concluded that warning from them to the people on the east side of the Sound was due. Indians upon whom they could rely were called in, and as a result a canoe was got ready in the darkness of the night for the fourteen-mile trip across the stormy waters. Sally, the daughter of old Chief Kitsap, said also to have been a cousin of Angeline, was captain, and under her were five other women and one man. Mrs. Maynard was the one passenger, she going as a courier or messenger to convey word of the threatened attack upon the town. The wind blew fiercely that night. The waves rolled high. With all their strength and skill the Indians could hardly keep their frail vessel afloat and moving. At one time they were blown upon West Point. Hostile Indians were there, and they examined the party. Finding that they were women and only one man they let them go. Before doing so, however, they inquired what was under the mats on the bottom of the canoe. Sally told them clams. In truth, it was Mrs. Maynard secreted there by Sally when she found that they were in danger. After a hard struggle the canoe was placed alongside the Decatur. Mrs. Maynard told the men on guard that she must see Capt. Gansevoort. He was wakened and acquainted with her and the object of her visit. She gave him a letter from Agent Maynard. The Captain had hot coffee and food provided for the Indians, and he urged Mrs. Maynard to stay at least until daylight. She said no, that she must be back by six in the morning, before daylight, so that her trip would not be known among the reservation Indians. On the return the wind blew harder than before, but it was a stern wind, and though dangerous, did not prevent arrival of the party before dawn. When the guns of the Decatur were heard booming an hour or two later, Chief Seattle was in great distress, and made pitiful demonstrations of the anguish he was in. He always felt his responsibility for the Indians under him, and he was sure now that it was a serious moment with them. Nor did he want his white friends hurt. That the differences between the two races would pass away gradually and easily was his hope and prayer. Nearly half a century later a bill was introduced in Congress by Representative J. H. Lewis to give Mrs. Maynard one thousand dollars as compensation for her hazardous and extraordinary services on this occasion. The bill, tho, did not pass. So firm was Gov. Stevens in the conviction that there was no longer danger from the Indians at this point that, upon his return, on the 27th, he was quite incredulous, and could hardly be made to believe that the day before they had attacked the fortified and garrisoned town of Seattle, and that had it not been for the protection afforded by the warship, her great guns and one hundred and fifty men, they possibly might have overcome the citizens, destroyed the place and massacred all the people, about two hundreds jn number.

It was real heroism that led Mrs. Maynard to doubly risk her life at this time. She had little chance against the' gale she was facing, and none whatever against the savages had she but fallen into their hands. How near she came to the latter mishap has been related. Only sheer necessity; the strong love she bore to her neighbors and friends in the town; the desire she had to frustrate the wicked plans of the hostile Indians, knowledge of which had come to her; could have nerved her to run the risks and make the effort required of her in this undertaking. That she was entirely successful is one of the happy events in the history of Seattle. Mrs. Maynard's life upon the reservation in January, 1856, was not so assured, comfortable and cheerful as may be imagined. Early in the month John Swan, agent near Steilcoom, was captured by Chief Leschi, who told him that he was after other agents as well. One of these was reported to be Maynard. Before he could accomplish this purpose, however, Leschi was driven back into the timber on the east side. Owhi was on Lake Washington at the time with a band of Yakimas and Klikitats, plotting, scheming and working for the destruction of the settlements. His emissaries were sent in every direction among the friendly Indians for the purpose of inciting them to deeds of violence like unto his own. Over and over again they appeared on the Port Madison reservation. Word of their presence was always brought to the Maynards by order of Seattle, with advice to keep indoors, to extinguish their lights and take other precautions. The Doctor never went out of evenings without being done up in a blanket, disguised as one of the tribe. His wife was dressed like a squaw for weeks. They had no fear of the Suquamish Indians—of Seattle, Angeline, Sally and the others—but they knew not at what moment they might come in contact with the Robbers (the meaning of Klikitats) of Eastern Washington, who were desperate, devilish and dangerous. A few days before the attack upon the town of Seattle three of these Klikitat warriors and one woman arrived on the reservation. As usual, their coming created a tremendous sensation. It soon became reported that they were there for the purpose of assassinating Chief Seattle and Agent Maynard; their idea being that as a result of the uproar that would follow the warship Decatur, and possibly some of the citizens of

111

the town, would be sent there to quiet and settle the disorder, and that their absence would give favorable opportunity for attacking and taking the town. Whether true or not, the report greatly excited the reservation Indians, who at once seized their weapons and started out in defense of their chief. The Klikitats became alarmed and fled, getting to their canoe, and paddling away rapidly as they could for Shilshole bay. About the same time there came report of another affair of unpleasant character. Gov. Stevens, as commander-in-chief of the Territorial forces, endeavored to array Indians against Indians, for the protection of his own countrymen. Companies were organized to fight the hostiles, and as inducement to them and compensation for their services, rewards were offered for the slaying of the enemies. It is said that one hundred dollars was the price for each dead Indian. Patkanim, chief of the Snoqualmies, who was bitterly opposed to Leschi, accepted a commission of this kind. For the purpose of seeing that he did what was right he was accompanied for a time by M. T. Simmons, Luther M. Collins, Truman H. Fuller and others. His warfare was not of the most approved kind, was timid when it should have been brave, was noisy when it should have been quiet and was ineffective when it should have been full of accomplishment. At one time he had some captives, or he pretended to have, and to get his pay killed the unfortunates in the most cold-blooded manner imaginable. In the presence of Col. Simmons he had five of them laid out on the ground. With sharp knives and axes he cut off their heads, which he threw into a sack, as a farmer would throw in rutabaga turnips, and then sent them to the Governor as proof of the justice of his demand for pay. It was with good reason suspected at the time that the slaughtered Indians were slaves that Patkanim had had in his, custody for years, who perhaps had outlived their usefulness, and whose disposal of in this way would be quite advantageous to the Snoqualmie chief. With such stories in circulation, and with the excitements and wild scenes about her, it is astonishing that Mrs. Maynard could have done what she did on this occasion. Few women would have been equal to the demand, and not many men. A full measure of credit should be awarded to her by the community she then so faithfully served.

THE Doctor and Mrs. Maynard stayed on the reservation a year and a half. Soon after their return to town exchange was made with Charles C. Terry of the unplatted portion of the Doctor's claim for Terry's claim at Alki Point. The Maynards got more land, but Terry got more value. For six years the Alki place was occupied, Dr. Maynard trying to do fine farming, and his wife keeping the house in good style, and helping outside when able. Both were glad to get back to town in 1863, where the old life was resumed with such modifications as were necessitated by the changed condition of affairs; the town having grown, the University being established, a newspaper started, a number of steamboats appearing, the Freeport and Blakely sawmills building nearby, many new settlers in town and country, and other signs and evidences of growth and development that gave proof to them of the correctness of their location ideas in 1852-3. In the first King County fair, held about this time, Mrs. Maynard entered a number of articles of her handiwork. The cake contest was quite spirited, but the premium was awarded to her. In 1867, November 15th, her brother, Col. M. T. Simmons, died at his home in Lewis County, respected as his distinguished services to the Territory justified. She and her husband then made an extended visit to his (Simmons's) family and home. From the earliest years Dr. Maynard had cared for the maimed and sick, at his dwelling, or in so-called hospitals, his wife always assisting, and becoming by her practise there as nurse, and by her observation and study, a good deal of a physician herself. So strong has been her leaning in that direction that to this day she has not been able to restrain a propensity to "doctor" all her- friends, advising them, prescribing for them, and even compounding medicines for them, in the effort to cure the ills from which they were suffering. The home of the Maynards was in the middle of the block on the east side of First Avenue South between Main and Jackson streets. There they lived until his death in 1873, and there she lived a number of years longer. The last thing she did there was to start a free reading room. In a large, light apartment, opening on the street, she placed tables and chairs, procured books, magazines and

114

newspapers, and invited the public to use them. For a year or more, in 1875-6, Mrs. Maynard kept the place open, clean, warm and pleasant. Her example had effect with others, the result being the establishment of the Young Men's Christian Association by Dexter Horton and associates, who took from Mrs. Maynard the burden she had carried so long. The magnificent tree and fine fruit that have come from the seed thus planted by this poor woman are known to all. "The widow's mite" was greater for good than the proud wealth of many of her townsmen. Her health had become weakened in the meantime, and, under the pressure of necessity for a change, she went to Eastern Washington. For about twenty years she dwelt alternately at Ellensburg, Medical Lake and Seattle, making her trips over the mountains on horseback as though she were a young woman of 20 to 40 years instead of the mature woman of 60 to 80. Her appearance on these occasions, riding gaily on her pony up to the homes of the McDonalds on Second avenue near Columbia street, the Meydenbauers, at Third and Columbia, the Kelloggs, at Fourth and Madison, and other of the first families, cannot be forgotten by her old-time friends.

DURING the past ten years she has been living quietly in Seattle, at the corner of Cherry street and Broadway. Notwithstanding her age and frailties she is yet a woman of considerable activity. She has made many pairs of socks, slippers and mittens for sale since her 80th year. She has done much fine needle work, in which she has few equals and no superiors. These tasks she does without the help of glasses. She gets out on the street shopping, to church, to the public grounds and to see her old friends and neighbors several times a week. She has a strong and clear memory of past events and people, which and whom she freely recalls in ordinary conversation. She does not care much for new people, and once in a while resents their intrusion in plain words and striking manner. Not long ago a nice looking, white-haired woman of about seventy years, called upon her, introducing herself pleasantly, saying she had heard much of Mrs. Maynard, wanted to know her, and had taken the liberty of coming. Being hard of hearing, it is possible Mrs. Maynard did not fully understand her, as she said to her visitor: "I do not feel like talking, and I may as well tell you that if you insist upon talking to me every word I say in reply will cost you 25 cents, and it will take a short time only to run up a charge against you of $25." The visiting lady did not care for conversation under such circumstances, and her first call was not only a short one but was also her last. The pioneers of the State, of course, are all interested in Mrs. Maynard, and she in them. Every annual meeting of the association finds her present. She is a veteran among them. No other member of the organization can equal her in the three claims of fifty-six years residence in the State, seventy- four years since her marriage, and ninety years of life. At the annual renuions the newspaper reporters and photographers are eager to get something from her. That she may continue to dwell among them happily and usefully for many years yet to come, is the sincere wish of her numerous friends in the great city which she helped to found and build and sustain, as partially narrated in these few pages.

POSTSCRIPT—NOVEMBER, 1906.

SINCE the foregoing was written and published (in June and July last), the end has come. Mrs. Maynard is no more. October 15th, in good spirits and in good condition, considering her age and physical weaknesses, she was out several hours, visiting neighbors and attending to personal affairs, among other things looking for a house upon the Maynard land claim within which to make her home. The weather was not pleasant. The wind blew, the rain fell, the temperature was low. With the dauntless spirit that possessed her, and with that determination for which she was noted, she kept on, regardless of her individual comfort and of the danger to which she was exposing her frail health. She went too far. She was out too long. She overtaxed herself. When she returned to the little house, at 1223 Cherry street, her strength was spent and she was able to do no more. The next morning she arose as usual, tottered around a few minutes, and fell to the floor in a condition of collapse, unconsciousness and paralysis being combined. Nearly four days she lingered, in a condition of coma, the physician, the nurse, the housekeeper, the friends being unable to do for her more than to make her comfortable. Just before her departure for the spirit land, and while apparently fully aware of her approaching dissolution, she emerged from unconsciousness long enough to say to Mrs. Hill, who for two years had been living with her: "Farewell; a last farewell." Shortly after, with the going down of the sun, on Saturday evening, Oct. 20th, 1906, she passed away. Her age was 90 years, 3 months, 1 day.

The newspapers—the Times and the Post-Intelligencer— next morning had much to say about her. Each of these great journals had two columns concerning this remarkable, this historic woman. Of none of the pioneers of the past was more said, or better. Their articles were illustrated with her portrait. They honored her memory in a manner quite gratifying to her acquaintances and friends. So they also treated the ceremonies connected with the final laying away of her remains.

On the 23d was the funeral. After a short service at the house in which she had so long dwelt, conducted by the Rev. A. L. Chapman, pastor of the church to which she belonged, the procession of carriages and people proceeded to the First Christian church, on Broadway and East Olive streets, where Was gathered one of the largest assemblages of people ever seen in Seattle on such an occasion. Among the number were •many of. Seattle's oldest and most venerable citizens, such as John Wilson, J. R. Williamson, Edgar Bryan, Theodore O. Williams, F. M. Guye, Samuel Jackson, Mrs. Bagley, Mrs. Boardman, Mrs. Meydenbauer, Mrs. Edwards, Mrs. Venen, Mrs. McLain, Mrs. Parker, Mrs. Dyer, Mrs. Shorey, Mrs. Randolph, Mrs. McElroy, John M. Lyon and wife, Walter Graham and wife, David

Graham and wife, George F. Frye and wife, and Charles Prosch and wife. Rev. George F. Whitworth, President of the Washington Pioneer Association, himself, like Mrs. Maynard, in his 91st year, assisted the pastor. He spoke most feelingly of his late friend, whom he had known for half a century, and dwelt particularly upon her services to the people of this city during the Indian war of 55-56. Coming from such a source, and spoken with such earnestness and sincerity, the words of Mr. Whitworth were impressive indeed. Rev. B. H. Lingenfelter, who had ministered to Mrs. Maynard several years before the coming of Mr. Chapman, told of her religious life. Mrs. Maynard joined the Baptist church in 1834. In 1847 she transferred her religious allegiance to the Christian church. This denomination being unrepresented in Seattle until a comparatively recent date, she had temporarily associated with the Congregationalists. She had been wonderfully faithful to her church attending its services whenever she was physically able so to do, seldom failing, and being one of the regular contributors to its support. No one in the congregation was better known, none more respected, and none would be more missed.

The services at the grave were brief and fitting. Under a canopy, they were conducted by Messrs. Chapman and Lingenfelter. The body was laid beside that of her husband, Doctor David S. Maynard, in Lakeview cemetery. A wealth of beautiful flowers covered the grave, contributed by those who had known her long and well. One of the finest floral offerings was from the King County Medical Society, which took this method of publicly recognizing the fact that she was the widow of Seattle's first physician, and further, that she herself was the first woman here to engage in hospital work. Another like graceful acknowledgment was from the Young Men's Christian Association, in token of her work thirty years before that led to the organization of the society, now so strong, so benevolent, so useful and helpful as theirs. Others who sent flowers were Mrs. Ursula Wyckoff, Mrs. S. J. Plummer, Mrs. G. O. Haller, Mrs. A. A. Denny, Mrs. P. Paulson, Mrs. M. E. Shorey, Mrs. T. W. Prosch, Mrs. G. Kellogg, Mrs. E. W. McGinness, Mrs. A. Mackintosh, Mrs. I. C. Parker, Mrs. R. B. Jones, Mrs. Quackenbush, and Mrs. Moore. Six pioneers were the pall-bearers, namely: Isaac C. Parker, Lyman W. Bonney, Clarence B. Bagley, F. H. Whitworth, S. P. Randolph and Leander Miller.

And thus, surrounded by friends who evidenced in every way their respect and regard, was laid to rest all that was mortal of one of the first women of this country, one who had lived long beyond the ordinary allotted time, one who had seen much of change and progress, and who had figured prominently in times and events that meant much to this community, and that will insure her memory among those who here projected and established what has become the State of Washington.

THE END.

Get more great reading from BIG BYTE BOOKS

Made in the USA
Coppell, TX
25 March 2020

17679718R10080